My God Time

Volume 1

MARGARET FEATHERSTONE

My God Time: Volume 1

Copyright 2020 by Margaret Featherstone. All rights reserved.

No part of this publication may be reproduced, stored in a retrieval system, or transmitted in any way, by any means whether electronically, mechanically, via photocopy, recording, or otherwise without the prior written permission of the publisher except as provided by USA copyright law.

Publishing assistance provided by TJS Publishing House
www.tjspublishinghouse.com
IG: @ tjspublishinghouse
FB: @ tjspublishinghouse
tjspublishinghouse@gmail.com

Cover design by TJS Publishing House

Published in the United States of America
ISBN-13: 978-1-952833-18-2
ISBN-10: 1-952833-18-3

DEDICATION

In memory of my Mom, who always dreamed of being a writer, and to my four sweet children and their generations to come.

CONTENTS

1	The Gospel of John	1
2	Acts of the Apostles	12
3	Paul's Letter to the Church in Rome	34
4	Paul's 1st Letter to the Church in Corinth	61
5	Paul's 2nd Letter to the Church in Corinth	79
6	Paul's Letter to the Church in Galatia	95
7	Paul's Letter to the Church in Ephesus	105
8	Paul's Letter to the Church in Philippi	119
9	Paul's Letter to the Church in Colossae	125
10	Paul's 1st & 2nd Letters to Timothy	130
11	The Book of Hebrews	143
12	The Book of James	161

ACKNOWLEDGMENTS

I want to thank God for calling me to spend time with Him. I also thank my husband and four children who encourage me, inspire me, and who give me the time and space I need to spend with God.

Introduction - The Back Story

The First Two Years

In fall of 2014, I had a strong sense of duty to spend time each day reading the Bible. No one shamed me into it or anything like that. I just felt such a strong push in my spirit to do this, an urge so strong I just had to obey it. At the time, I was a very busy mother of four, working full-time. My oldest child had just married, I had one away at college, one starting high school, and the little one was still in elementary school. It wasn't like I really had extra time to do this, but I felt that I had to, that I had no choice, that it was important. I wanted to know God. I felt I needed a more solid relationship with Jesus, and I hoped that spending time in his word would fill this void inside me.

For two years, I read the Bible regularly, albeit not every day. I set out to read every day, but I slipped up here and there in the busyness of life. Sometimes I could only read for five minutes, while other times I could read for much longer. Whenever I read, I would read until something popped off the page for me, or really caught my attention. I would then immediately write down the thoughts flooding my mind with regard to that passage. Often it felt like my pen couldn't write fast enough to keep up with my mind, and my hurried handwriting was often barely legible. Other times it was just a short note. I felt that God was teaching me important truths that I needed to learn and remember.

Years Three and Four

After two years of writing, I started typing up the notes I had written. This undertaking was driven by a fear that I would forget some of what I had written and eventually wouldn't be able to read my own handwriting! I really wanted to preserve these moments I had had with God in His word. I wondered why I had written all of this, experienced all of this. I thought there was a substantial purpose in all of this reading and writing, but I wasn't sure what it was. Were these two years of writing just for my own growth, or was I meant to share it? I thought maybe I should share it with my children. I decided to type up all the notes in preparation for perhaps binding it into a book of some type they could keep and pass on to their children. My hope was that this might keep them close to God or at least spark within them an interest in His word.

The Blog

In March 2019, I sensed that the Lord was asking me to share our times together to a wider audience than just my family, that I should share it through a blog page. At first, I thought this was a great idea, and then it terrified me. It's a little scary thinking about sharing your innermost thoughts with the whole world—not to mention that I had no experience with the software or any of the skills I needed to set this up. However, I continued to receive confirmation that this was what I needed to do, so I started blogging My God Time in April 2019.

The Book

In April 2020, I had been publishing on my blog for an entire year, and I felt the nudge to finally turn the project into a book. In these pages, you will find a copy of my blog entries from April 2019 to April 2020, covering the Journal Entries I made between October 2014 and August 2015. My hope is that the book will inspire your personal journey with God. After all, if a regular person like me can grow in my relationship with the God of the Universe, so can you! You really do have a unique role in God's Kingdom and in this amazing family of God. Please accept the gift Jesus died to give you – the opportunity to get to know God, the one who created you and loves you more than you will ever comprehend.

SPRING

1
THE GOSPEL OF JOHN

What Place Does Jesus Have in Your Life?
1st Journal Entry   17 October 2014
Blog Entry   12 April 2019

John 5 – Jesus heals the man at the pool but requires that he participates in the healing. You have to be in it as well. God could do it by Himself, but needs you to actively participate. Your participation allows you to learn the things you need to learn as you advance in His kingdom and grow to the next level of understanding His plan for your life.

John 7 – People who don't take Jesus seriously can't believe He's really the Son of God. His brothers ridicule him. The Pharisees try to trap him. All of Jesus' actions, the healings, and wisdom He has, are screaming out that He is the long-awaited Messiah. Yet, everyone is finding excuses not to believe. You weren't born in Bethlehem; you're just plain old Jesus from Galilee. Do we also only give Him that place in our lives? Do we make him small and insignificant, or do we truly acknowledge who He is and what He did for us?

Choose to Walk in the Light
Journal Entry   19 October 2014
Blog Entry   15 April 2019

Jesus spoke to the people once more and said, "I am the light of the world. If you follow me, you won't have to walk in darkness, because you will have the light that leads to life." (John 8:12 NLT)

You can have, you will have, such an enlightened life, seeing things you wouldn't have seen, making decisions you wouldn't have made, if you are doing your best to follow Christ. All these decisions will make your life better, brighter, freer, and more wonderful! But you miss all that if you choose not to follow.

He Doesn't Condemn Us
Journal Entry   20 October 2014
Blog Entry 17   April 2019

In John 8:1-11, we read the story of the woman they wanted to stone, whom Jesus saved by telling them that the one with no sin should cast the first stone. A revelation I had while reading this was not focused so much on the judgment the others were having on the woman; the lesson about not judging others. What I learned this time was about the very end of the story, the part where Jesus says, "neither do I condemn you." So although He is the only one with the right to condemn us, He chooses not to.

Update - 17 April 2019

That's one of the things I love about the Bible. The Holy Spirit can show you something new every time you read it. It's not like other books you read. If you ask the Holy

Spirit to reveal new things to you, He will. There's a relationship that is happening in your spirit when you are reading, and God is actually speaking to you, showing you things. On this particular day, back in October 2014, God wanted me to know that He chooses to love me and forgive me for every mistake I will ever make. Even though He has every right to condemn me, He won't.

Walk in Freedom
Journal Entry   21 October 2014
Blog Entry   19 April 2019

Jesus said to the people who believed in him, "You are truly my disciples if you remain faithful to my teachings. ³² And you will know the truth, and the truth will set you free." (John 8:31 NLT)

As long as you stay as close as you can to God, know and follow His teachings, you will experience a kind of freedom that you cannot get from anything else.

Update - 19 April 2019

Today is Good Friday. I woke up thinking how thankful I am to Jesus for going to the cross for me. I said, "Thank you, Jesus." But I knew such a sentiment was so inadequate, that there are no words or anything I can offer good enough for what He did for me. Then I thought I'll spend my life obeying God's word and doing my best to be Jesus's hands and feet in the world in order to thank Him. Then I heard Him tell me that doing that would be *works*, and His gift is free. I'm sure He would like me to obey God's word and be His hands and feet, as that would make my life even better, and He wants me to have an abundant life; but I don't have to do those things to pay Him back. His gift to us is free. We just need to receive it.

Can You Hear Him?
Journal Entry   22 October 2014
Blog Entry   22 April 2019

Anyone who belongs to God listens gladly to the words of God. But you don't listen because you don't belong to God. (John 8:47 NLT)

The story that precedes this verse is one in which Jesus tells them that they are not truly the children of Abraham. At least, they are not *spiritually* the children of Abraham, because if they were, they would believe and understand what He was telling them. Their eyes would be open to the truth if they were truly God's children. The veil of mystery and understanding would be lifted. Since they hadn't chosen to believe, they remained children of the devil, the father of all lies, and were unable to hear the truth. You can't start to hear the truth until you make that all-important choice to believe by faith.

Choosing to Remain Spiritually Blind
Journal Entry   23 October 2014
Blog Entry   24 April 2019

In the Ninth Chapter of John, we have the story about a man who was born blind. Jesus uses mud to heal him. Since the man was born blind, the people asked if this was because of his sin or his parent's sin. Jesus says neither; he was born blind to glorify God.

An interesting concept it is that not all things we see as imperfections are due to sin, but some are there to glorify God. In this case, the man's blindness was available to be used by Jesus to show people the difference between spiritual blindness and spiritual sight.

This healing was used to teach the Pharisees. The blind man knew he was healed by God's power, so he believed

Jesus was from God. The Pharisees could also clearly see this is what happened. However, they chose to continue in their spiritual blindness.

Then Jesus told him (the blind man), "I entered this world to render judgment—to give sight to the blind and to show those who think they see that they are blind." Some Pharisees who were standing nearby heard him and asked, "Are you saying we're blind?" "If you were blind, you wouldn't be guilty," Jesus replied. "But you remain guilty because you claim you can see." (John 9:39-41 NLT)

In other words, the Pharisees knew God had healed the man through Jesus, but they refused to believe it. They didn't want to acknowledge who Jesus was, the son of God, and give up their "authority". They weren't spiritually blind, in that they did see the truth, but they refused to accept it.

Judas's Betrayal
Journal Entry   24 October 2014
Blog Entry   26 April 2019

In reading the account of Judas's betrayal, I realized that Jesus knew what Judas was going to do, but maybe Judas did not realize what would happen because of his actions.

Now Jesus was deeply troubled, and he exclaimed, "I tell you the truth, one of you will betray me!" (John 13:21 NLT)

Judas was one of the most trusted disciples, so much so that they trusted him with the money. Judas may have been very loyal to the cause, but thought he could force Jesus' hand to set up His kingdom on earth by turning Him over to the Pharisees.

Judas knew what Jesus was capable of, so maybe he didn't realize his actions would end in Jesus' death. Maybe it wasn't as straightforward as it seems. Maybe it wasn't just for the money. Maybe Judas's motives weren't all bad, but Satan used his thinking, which was contrary to God's way, to set in motion the events that would lead to Jesus' death.

We always think of Judas as a traitor, but perhaps it wasn't that simple. Maybe Judas thought Jesus could rescue Himself and claim His rightful place as King. There are other scriptures that say Judas was a thief, so yes, he was in it for the money, but at the very least, it is possible he didn't realize his actions would lead to Jesus' death.

After his mistake, Judas could have still received Jesus' forgiveness if he had chosen to do so. However, he couldn't forgive himself, and that's the real tragedy. Maybe Judas could have gone on to become a powerful saint like Paul, but he didn't.

What is the lesson here? Trust God afresh, even after you've made terrible mistakes, and He will redeem your life. We are going to make mistakes, even when we are trying to do good or do what we think will help the Kingdom. But we need to accept God's forgiveness when we go wrong so He can use us afresh again and again.

The Vine and the Branches
Journal Entry   3 November 2014
Blog Entry   29 April 2019

When you produce much fruit, you are my true disciples. This brings great glory to my Father. (John15:8 NLT)

I often feel guilty that I don't overtly give Jesus credit for good things I do. I feel like others praise me, and I don't immediately tell them that it's God's Spirit working in me, not me, that accomplishes these things. I carry a lot of guilt about that. I prayed about it just this morning before my Bible time, that God would work through me so that people will see Him and not me.

I feel that the Lord spoke to me this morning through John 15:8, telling me not to worry, that He is glorified when I produce good fruit in my life. He is glorified even if it's not always announced out loud that He's the reason for the fruit. I am continually glorifying God by the life I am living, remaining faithful to Him. Living life this way in itself glorifies God. I must not allow the enemy of my soul to make me feel ashamed and feel less than what I am. I am a child of God! I have been chosen by God to do His good works in the world.

I no longer call you slaves, because a master doesn't confide in his slaves. Now you are my friends, since I have told you everything the Father told me. [16] You didn't choose me. I chose you. I appointed you to go and produce lasting fruit, so that the Father will give you whatever you ask for, using my name. (John 15:15-16 NLT)

The World's Hatred for Christians
Journal Entry   4 November 2014
Blog Entry   1 May 2019

"If the world hates you, remember that it hated me first. [19] The world would love you as one of its own if you belonged to it, but you are no longer part of the world. I chose you to come out of the world, so it hates you. [20] Do you remember what I told you? 'A slave is not greater than the master.' Since they persecuted me, naturally they will persecute you. And if they had listened to me, they would listen to you. [21] They will do all this to you because of me, for they have rejected the one who sent me. [22] They would not be guilty if I had not

come and spoken to them. But now they have no excuse for their sin."
(John15:18-23 NLT)

The world hates and rejects Christians because we don't belong to the world; we belong to God. All the people in the world also belong to God and know in their hearts that the right decision is to love and follow God, but they choose to reject God. Therefore, when they see those who are following God, they hate them because they know this is what they should be doing as well. It is our light that highlights their darkness.

The Temple Guards Arrest Jesus
Journal Entry   7 November 2014
Blog Entry   3 May 2019

In John 18:1-10, we have the account of the temple guards coming to arrest Jesus. My Life Application Bible notes really spoke to me today. They noted that the arrest of Jesus was a turning point for Jesus' disciples. This was the first time Judas openly betrayed Jesus in front of the others. They all scattered after the arrest, partly because Jesus said to let them go. Now they had to decide where to go from here. From this point on, each of them underwent severe testing in order that they could be transformed from hesitant followers to dynamic leaders! Don't we all have to pass these tests?

Update 3 May 2019

In reading John 18:1-10 today, I was struck by verse six. The soldiers march through the dark with Judas, torches blazing, swords readied. They are on the hunt for Jesus. Jesus knows they are coming to get him, and when they arrive, He asks whom they are looking for. After they tell him, He answers, saying, "I am He." It's what happens after this that I hadn't noticed before:

⁶ As Jesus said, "I am he," they all drew back and fell to the ground! (John18:6 NLT)

I think that they couldn't help drawing back and falling to the ground. That there was so much power when Jesus identified Himself that it knocked them all to their knees.

It reminds me of something personal that happened about twelve or thirteen years ago. I was a cast member in a play at a church we were attending. I was playing the part of a grandmother who had died and was walking up to meet Jesus in Heaven. When I walked up to meet the person playing Jesus, I was supposed to be in awe of Jesus' presence. During the actual production, when I started to walk up and he reached out his hand to greet me, I was genuinely struck with awe and wonder and fell to my knees. It was such an amazing experience.

I realize of course that I wasn't actually meeting Jesus, but just the actor playing Him, but it was as if I got a glimpse of what it will be like when I do meet Him. I couldn't even play my part in this scene without feeling some of the power of His presence. I believe there is so much power around Him that no one will be able to stand up. It brought to mind the scriptures, *"Every knee will bow and tongue confess that He is Lord." (Isaiah 45:23, Romans 14:11, Philippians 2:10)* When we meet Jesus, we won't have a choice to bow. We will fall at His feet.

Jesus on Trial
Journal Entry   11 November 2014
Blog Entry   6 May 2019

"Why don't you talk to me?" Pilate demanded. "Don't you realize that I have the power to release you or crucify you?" Then Jesus said, "You would have no power over me at all unless it were given to you

from above..." (John 19:10 NLT)
Jesus was in control during the whole trial. Those who thought they were in control of the situation and had "the power" were actually the ones on trial.

When people persecute you about your beliefs, they are actually on trial with God. Stand firm in your love and commitment to God when those times come. Don't waiver from your solid grounding and knowledge of the truth! Reflect on Jesus' attitude when He was on trial. Rest assured of all you know to be true.

Jesus' Death and Resurrection
Journal Entry   12 November 2014
Blog Entry   8 May 2019

John Chapters 19 & 20 describe Jesus' death on the cross and also His resurrection. Jesus had to suffer so much, more than we can imagine, to achieve freedom and new life for us. How happy He must have been that He had accomplished His goal! He had made it through the trials, temptations, and now He was free forever!

The example Jesus set for us helps us to see what it means to take up your cross (Matt 10:28, Matt 16:34, Mark 8:34, Luke 9:23). We have to resist the temptations in this world to achieve our place of freedom. Everyone struggles with their own unique temptations in life, the things that pull them away from the path God is calling them to follow. I also think the temptations change over the years. I've had many different challenges and temptations in my lifetime. One temptation I need to overcome is overeating and lack of exercise. Overcoming these temptations will lead to my freedom from this overweight, tired body to one of renewed energy and life!

Another thought I had while reading John 19 and 20 is that we didn't choose Jesus; He chose us. He initiated the relationship. It's not about us. It's about Him. It's not about me going to Him. It's about allowing Him to draw near to me. He's the leader, the initiator of the relationship. I just have to choose to follow, to receive, and to submit. My default is to see things as if I'm in charge. I need to work on that, particularly in my relationship with Jesus. I need to realize He is leading and allow Him to lead me.

The Resurrected Jesus Speaking to His Disciples
Journal Entry   13 November 2014
Blog Entry   10 May 2019

Then he breathed on them and said, "Receive the Holy Spirit. (John 20:22 NLT)

Jesus breathes the Holy Spirit into us so that we can have a new life here on earth, so we can accomplish great things that we cannot do in our own strength. I need to remember not to strive in my own strength but to trust God and lean on Him, turn to Him, ask for help.

Peter asked Jesus, "What about him, Lord?"
^{22} Jesus replied, "If I want him to remain alive until I return, what is that to you? As for you, follow me." (John 21:21-22 NLT)

God gives us each our own special, unique mission. We should not be envious of other's missions but focus on our own tasks and be thankful for the mission He has chosen for us. He has designed us specifically for the mission he has planned for us. We may discover talents and abilities even in older age that we didn't know we had, as he equips us for the work He has for us to do.

2
ACTS OF THE APOSTLES

Pentecost and the Holy Spirit
Journal Entry   14 November 2014
Blog Entry   13 May 2019

In the Book of Acts, Chapter 2, we read about the Holy Spirit coming at Pentecost, 40 days after Jesus' Resurrection. The Spirit gave all the followers of Jesus the ability to speak in different languages. This miracle gave them the opportunity to spread the Gospel message in the native languages of all the people gathered there. I've always thought of this particular outpouring of the Holy Spirit in that specific way. However, while reading the passage today, God revealed to me that the Holy Spirit also gives you the ability to speak to others about God in a way they will understand, even if you both speak the same language.

Peter's Speech

Acts 2:14 to 41 offers the account of Peter's speech at Pentecost. Peter gets up and shouts to address the crowd with an amazing speech. Peter had always been a bit of a loudmouth. Previously, that trait had gotten him into trouble as he denied knowing Jesus when he had promised to never do such a thing. But this characteristic, this boldness, was still part of who he was, and the Holy Spirit turned it around on this day to be used for good.

Using our Unique Abilities
We are who we are genetically. We all have our own unique personalities, gifts, abilities, and hangups. If we really want to make full use of who we are, who we were created to be, we need the Holy Spirit to empower us to do that. Otherwise, we end up wasting our gifts or using

them other than the way God intended for us when He created us. This will only leave us feeling dissatisfied with our lives, no matter what we achieve in our human strength.

Healing of the Crippled Man
Journal Entry   17 November 2014
Blog Entry   15 May 2019

In Acts Chapter 3, we read of the healing of a man who had been unable to walk for forty years. After reading about the healing in Chapter 3, then Peter's message in Chapter 4, I felt that, like the crippled man, I had access to the healing power of God. I felt that God was beginning to heal me from many things and was also beginning to heal my body from overweight and overeating after 40 years of neglect.

"Starting with Samuel, every prophet spoke about what is happening today. [25] You are the children of those prophets, and you are included in the covenant God promised to your ancestors. For God said to Abraham, 'Through your descendants all the families on earth will be blessed.' [26] When God raised up his servant, Jesus, he sent him first to you people of Israel, to bless you by turning each of you back from your sinful ways." (Acts 3:24-26 NLT)

Jesus was sent first to the people of Israel but also to the Gentiles, as we all need to be healed from our sinful ways, and we need His help to do it! We can't do these things and make the changes we need to in our own strength. I realize that I can bring Him glory as people begin to see changes in me and that I need to tell people about God's part in these changes.

Dear God, in Jesus' name, teach me how to give you glory for the changes you are making in me! Give me the words to glorify You whenever people notice a change in me that you have made.

Ananias and Sapphira
Journal Entry   18 November 2014
Blog Entry   17 May 2019

Acts 5:1-10 recounts the story of a man named Ananias and his wife, Sapphira. They sold some of their property and brought some of the money to contribute to the growing group of believers. This was a great thing, but what they did wrong was that they lied about how much of the profit they had given to the group. For me, the moral of this story is that it's not a sin to be stingy, but it's a sin to brag about how much you give to the church, especially if you exaggerate about how much you give to the church. It's a sin to lie to God and to God's people about your commitment to Him and to them.

The Apostles Healing Many People
Journal Entry   19 November 2014
Blog Entry   20 May 2019

But no one else dared to join them even though they had high regard for them (Acts 5:13)

The Apostles are teaching and performing miracles. Even Peter's shadow is healing people! The believers are meeting regularly, but others are afraid to join them. What does this mean? Why would they be afraid to join?

I spoke to my son Peter at breakfast about Acts 5:13 and the idea that people were afraid to join the group of believers. He thought it could be because it was new and different, and they didn't understand it, that it was a bit frightening and unfamiliar to them. I thought that was an awesome bit of wisdom from my fourteen-year-old son. Perhaps they were afraid that they weren't equipped to be disciples. I think a lot of us still do that, or have that kind of thinking. We think we are not good enough to be Christians. We think we need special qualifications or righteousness. We think of sinful things we do, even minor things, and believe this makes us unqualified to be a Christian. This is a lie from our enemy Satan to keep us separated from God.

Update - 20 May 2019

Writing this blog entry up today reminded me of something my mom said to me about twenty-five years ago. At that time, I was about four years into taking my faith more seriously and not just being a Christmas-and-Easter-only Christian. I had neighbours a couple of doors down who were solid believers. They held prayer meetings at their home and brought meals to people who were going through hardships, among other wonderful things. I was so impressed by them and wished I was more like them. At the time I felt inadequate. I was sure that I wasn't a "good enough" Christian. I was talking to my mom about it, and I remember saying to her that I wish I was more like them. She replied, "You are them." From her perspective, I was just as much a believer as they were. Although I wasn't yet doing some of the specific things they were doing, I was just as much a Christian. Those three words, *you are them*, really stuck with me. They actually shifted my perspective from that day on about who I was in Christ from "not good enough" to a growing branch in the body of Christ.

The Stoning of Stephen
Journal Entry   *20 November 2014*
Blog Entry   *22 May 2019*

I read Acts 6 and 7 today, learning about the apostles appointing administrators to run the food distribution, as well as Stephen's speech, stoning, and the impact that event had on Saul/Paul.

I learned that we each have an important role to play. Even if you think your part isn't important or doesn't seem important, it really is just as important as anyone else's part in the Kingdom of God.

The fact that Stephen remained faithful and asked God to forgive those you were killing him (even while they were killing him) had perhaps a greater impact on Saul, and therefore on all those Paul would reach in the future, than the words Stephen spoke in his powerful speech captured in Acts 7. I think Stephen's display of steadfast faith and forgiveness for those killing him had perhaps a greater impact than anything he did in his life.

We never know what part of our lives will be used to bring God glory. However, if we are open to God and ask Him to use us, He will. We all have to play our part so that others can be free to play their part or learn what they need to learn from us. We might never realize how powerfully God is using us as we carry out our responsibilities and live out our daily lives.

Simon the Magician
Journal Entry   21 November 2014
Blog Entry   24 May 2019

Acts 8:9-24 tells the story of Simon the magician, the lesson that it's **not** about me!

Simon wanted the gift of the Holy Spirit, even wanted to pay for it, so that he could become rich and successful. This story teaches us that we must shift our thinking off of ourselves and onto others.

I had a revelation yesterday, and was reminded of it today. I often want God's power for myself, for me to be more successful, powerful, influential, or financially well off. But it is important that I keep asking God to help me shift my thinking and change my motives to wanting, pursuing, needing God's power only to bless others, and not for myself.

God will always take care of me. I can trust in that. I need to focus first on others, not on myself. What can I do for them? This should be my daily motivation, my underlying motive for my life, and for all I do.

This was confirmed today at work. I was thinking of the big move we were about to go through into a new building and a new environment. We are going to have a new company taking care of our security instead of our older security staff that I've known for over thirty years. I found myself thinking poorly of the new young security guards instead of thinking of some way I could bless these new people I would be meeting. I was thinking that these kids better not give me a hard time as I had been with the organization for over thirty years. I should have been thinking about how daunting it must feel for these younglings to be charged with looking after us. I should have been thinking of ways to make them feel welcome as part of our big work family. Thank you, Father, for helping me to catch those thoughts and correct them!

Philip and the Eunuch and Saul's Conversion
Journal Entry   22 November 2014
Blog Entry   27 May 2019

Acts 8:26-39 Philip and the Ethiopian Eunuch
Philip met this man where he was and explained what the Gospel of Jesus meant in answer to the particular question the Eunuch asked. The Eunuch was reading from the

prophet Isaiah *(53:7-9 NLT)* and didn't understand what it meant.

He was led like a lamb to the slaughter.
  And as a sheep is silent before the shearers,
  he did not open his mouth.
Unjustly condemned,
  he was led away.
No one cared that he died without descendants,
  that his life was cut short in midstream.
But he was struck down
  for the rebellion of my people.
He had done no wrong
  and had never deceived anyone.
But he was buried like a criminal;
  he was put in a rich man's grave.

The eunuch asked Philip;
"Tell me, was the prophet talking about himself or someone else?" [35] *So beginning with this same Scripture, Philip told him the Good News about Jesus. (Acts 8:34-35 NLT)*

It's important to share the gospel with people from where they are. You don't need to go overboard telling them everything you know; just start with the little piece or spot they are trying to understand.

Acts 9: Saul's Conversion

Such an amazing chapter! Saul was determined to kill all the believers. He had obtained permission to round up all the believers in Damascus and bring them back to Jerusalem in chains. However, on his way, he met the risen Jesus and was transformed. Instead of continuing to persecute the believers, he became the chief of them.

After Saul met Jesus, his life was completely changed! We

meet the same Jesus Saul met, the risen Jesus, and our lives begin to change from that point forward as well!

Peter and Cornelius
Journal Entry   24 November 2014
Blog Entry   29 May 2019

Acts Chapter 10 recounts a story about Peter and a Roman Army Officer named Cornelius. Peter states in this story that God has shown him that he should no longer think of anyone as impure or unclean. The reason is, God sees everyone the same; we should never look down on anyone else but see them the way God does.

Then Peter replied, "I see very clearly that God shows no favouritism. ^{35} *In every nation he accepts those who fear him and do what is right. (Acts 10:34-35 NLT)*

I pray God that you help me do that. I confess that I do automatically think poorly of some people in society. Even though I don't want to think this way, I know that I do. Outwardly I believe I treat them well but help me change my heart and thinking so that I don't think less of them at all!

In Acts 10, Cornelius falls at Peter's feet and worships him when he meets him, but Peter says, "Get up, I'm not God but a human being just like you." I felt God tell me that this is the reason I like pastors who say they are just like us. Personally, it really resonates with me when a Pastor admits his faults and says he's no better than the rest of us.

I felt God instructing me that when I have the opportunity to spread the good news to others, I need to assure them that I'm no closer to God than they are. We are all the same! This is why "church people" should not feel superior to the unchurched. They aren't any "better" than unchurched folks; they've just been around church more often and might have more Bible and scripture knowledge.

Update - 29 May 2019

As I was reading Acts 10 this morning, verses 40 - 42 popped out at me:

They put him to death by hanging him on a cross [40] *but God raised him to life on the third day. Then God allowed him to appear,* [41] *not to the general public, but to us whom God had chosen in advance to be his witnesses. We were those who ate and drank with him after he rose from the dead.* [42] *And he ordered us to preach everywhere and to testify that Jesus is the one appointed by God to be the judge of all— the living and the dead. (Acts 10:40-42 NLT)*

When I read this, I felt a genuine call to be a witness to others, to tell them the Gospel message. I felt that if God allows some of us to hear and understand the Gospel message, then it becomes our responsibility to reach others with this truth. To be honest, I've always felt a little reluctant to reach out to others with the Gospel as I felt unqualified and didn't want to be "pushy". However, after reflecting on this passage, I feel that once we know the Gospel, if God allows us to understand this truth, He is trusting us to reach others with the message.

James is Killed. Peter is Put in Prison
Journal Entry   26 November 2014
Blog Entry   31 May 2019

In Acts Chapter 12, King Herod Agrippa has James killed, and puts Peter in prison.

King Herod Agrippa was trying to gain favour with the Jews by stamping out the Christian movement. In the NLT study notes, it asks, why did James have to die, and why was John spared?

This morning before reading, I was thinking about one of my children and how he has to work so hard to study for tests, whereas it comes much easier for some of my other kids. So this passage, and question in the study notes, made me think about these types of questions in life. Why does one child have certain gifts and another child not have these gifts? The NLT study notes go on to say that "God will use our suffering to strengthen us and glorify Him!"

I believe that God doesn't waste anything He creates. He has a purpose for every single one of us and every situation. If we just seek Him out, He will be strong where we are weak, and this ultimately brings Him glory.

Paul, Barnabas, and John Mark
Journal Entry   27 November 2014
Blog Entry   3 June 2019

In Acts Chapter 13, verses 4 to 13, John Mark starts off with Barnabas and Paul but then leaves. John Mark started off with Barnabas and Paul on Paul's first missionary journey as their assistant. However, after a short time with them, he left and went back to Jerusalem.

The message that popped out for me from this incident was that even when we fail, God continues to have mercy on us and encourages us to keep trying, to keep drawing close. He can still use us in mighty ways, even in our mistakes and weaknesses! He doesn't want us to give up or count our attempts to serve Him as useless or wrong. When our hearts are in the right place, God will use us, even if we feel that we have failed.

Paul and Barnabas on the First Missionary Journey

Journal Entry   28 November 2014
Blog Entry   5 June 2019

In Acts Chapters 13 and 14, we read the account of Paul and Barnabas on their First Missionary Journey. In each town, they would tell the Gospel story first to the Jewish people and then to the Gentiles.

Paul preaches to the Jewish people about Jesus. He starts with what they know, the history of the Jewish nation, and then teaches them about Jesus and how He fits into God's plan for them. I see this as a great model for us when we are telling people about Jesus. Always start with what your listeners understand, from where they are at in their faith.

Some towns received and understood the Gospel message. Some of the people in the towns received Paul's teaching with joy. Others rejected it, even when they saw amazing miracles God performed through Paul and Barnabas. In one town, they even stoned Paul and thought he was dead. But God ensured that he survived the stoning.

I felt God telling me not to get discouraged when sowing seeds of the Gospel message. Sew wherever you can and let the Holy Spirit grow it. My job is to plant. I'm not responsible for the growth. One phrase that caught my eye was, "some of them poisoned the minds of the others against Paul and Barnabas." We must be careful not to poison people's minds with negative talk about others. It's important to always be encouraging and build each other up, and not tear each other down.

Timothy, the First Second Generation Christian; and Lydia of Philipi, the First European Convert

Journal Entry   2 December 2014
Blog Entry   7 June 2019

Timothy

Acts 16:1-5 tells us that Timothy will travel with Paul and Silas on their missionary journey. Timothy is the first Second Generation Christian we hear about in the New Testament. His mother Eunice and grandmother Lois were believers. His father was an unbelieving Greek. The message for me here is that we should never underestimate the power of a believing mother!

Silas

Silas often accompanied Paul and was not as highly celebrated a figure in the Bible but nonetheless played out his role in planting seeds and bringing others to Christ. The message I'm hearing this morning is; don't underestimate the power of quiet and steady faith and how it will impact the world and others. Thank you, Holy Spirit, for giving me reassurance today that I am who you need me to be, doing what I need to be doing. That even though I struggle and fail many times that you see and know my steadfast faith and will use it for Your glory.

Lydia

Lydia of Philipi was the first European convert to believe in Christ. The Bible tells us that God opened her heart to believe. We can't believe without God allowing us to do so. I am so grateful that God has allowed me, my children, and my husband to believe! Please, God, continue to take us deeper in our relationship and commitment to you! Allow us to know you more and more!

Paul and Silas Sing Praises to God From a Prison Cell

Journal Entry   4 December 2014
Blog Entry   10 June 2019

In Acts Chapter 16, verses 19 to 25, we read that Paul and Silas are thrown into prison because Paul had cast a spirit of divination out of a slave girl. She could no longer make money for her master as she was no longer possessed by the spirit. Her masters accused Paul and Silas of acting unlawfully. Consequently, they were beaten and imprisoned. While in prison, even after being beaten and placed in stocks, they sang and praised God! This was a reminder to me to Praise God every day in all circumstances. He is working for your good, no matter what you are going through!

Paul and Silas in Thessalonica and Berea
Journal Entry   5 December 2014
Blog Entry   12 June 2019

Acts 17:1-15 describes the activities of Paul and Silas in the cities of Thessalonica and Berea. Paul and Silas were going into the Synagogues and using the Jewish scriptures to teach the Jewish people and new believers about Jesus. They showed them that the scriptures predicted exactly what had taken place and that the Messiah had come. They went about teaching the Jewish people and the Greeks this Good News!

Some of the people believed, but others formed groups to incite riots and run them out of town or get them thrown into jail for treason.

The thing that hit me this morning while reading was the idea that the people who didn't believe would "form groups" to get rid of the Apostles. I remember reading about this group mentality in other stories in the Book of Acts as well. It is also evident when Jesus was crucified and, the "crowd" was yelling to crucify Him. No one ever seemed to stand on their own to oppose the Apostles. While the Apostles usually spread the Good News alone, or by twos, those who opposed them would generally form groups to bring havoc and incite the crowd to violence against them.

I thought about this in the context of our world today with the ISIS movement and other hate groups. These "groups" that spread hatred and destruction do so from the basis of a group mentality. Whereas Christians spreading the Good News tend to do so from individual to individual. I Just found that kind of interesting.

Paul Spreads the Good News in Athens
Journal Entry   8 December 2014
Blog Entry   14 June 2019

Acts 17:16 to 34 - Paul in Athens
Paul sees that the Greeks want to understand who God is. He sees that they are religious and have even created an altar of worship to the unknown god. He preaches the Good News in Athens, telling them that he knows who this unknown God is and can tell them about Him. He tells them that God isn't made of things of the earth, as He Himself created these things. Paul says there was a time when God didn't call us to make our paths straight, that it was OK to be ignorant of who God really was, but now it was time to see and understand who the one true God really is. Now that Jesus had come, they were called to action, to listen to the voice of the Holy Spirit that dwelt inside of them!

Acts 18:9 and 18:20 - When to Go and When to Stay
One night in a vision, the Lord told Paul, "Do not be afraid! Speak out. Tell the truth about Jesus!" Our current series at church is titled *Fear Not,* and I think that God is telling me not to be afraid to speak of Him to my co-workers, that He will give me the words! Further, in 18:20, they asked Paul to stay, but he said he couldn't. I sensed a message in my spirit here that it's okay to say "No" sometimes. Even when you are doing good work, you

must go where God calls you to go, not where you think you should go!

Paul traveling and Apollos in Ephesus
Journal Entry   9 December 2014
Blog Entry   17 June 2019

Acts 18:18-23 - Paul in Corinth, Cenchrea, Syria, Ephesus, Caesarea, Antioch, Galatia, and Phrygia

Paul moves from place to place, spreading the Gospel message. He follows the lead of the Holy Spirit and says no when he doesn't think the Lord is leading him to a particular place. He waits on the Lord and follows what he believes God is telling him. He doesn't rush off in every direction, and he leaves a city or town only when he senses the Lord directing him to move on.

I think this is an important message God is teaching me. I need to slow down and allow God to lead. This idea reminds me of a Joyce Meyer statement I once heard. Joyce said she doesn't necessarily hear from God every day, so she just keeps doing the last thing He told her to do. I think that is very helpful advice. I just need to do the things He calls me to do, focus in on those things, and stop acting like I need to solve every problem for everyone in the world!

Acts 18:24-28 - Apollos

Apollos was a Greek Jew and eloquent speaker who had a thorough knowledge of the scriptures. He argued with the Pharisees, and other Jewish leaders, as he believed that Jesus was the Messiah. Originally, he only knew about John's baptism of repentance and not the baptism of the Holy Spirit. Priscilla and Aquila heard him speak in Ephesus and spoke to him afterward to enhance his understanding. Apollos went on to become a bold advocate for Christ and had a large following.

¹² *Some of you are saying, "I am a follower of Paul." Others are saying, "I follow Apollos," or "I follow Peter," or "I follow only Christ." (1 Corinthians 1:12 NLT)*

Unfortunately, some people became more enamoured with Apollos than with God, even though that was not his intention. This was starting to cause division within the church at Corinth, as some said they were following Paul, or Apollos, or Peter, or Christ. Paul tried to set them straight in telling them that there is one Christ, and they are to look to Jesus, not the messengers.

Dear God, help me to always glorify You in the world, and not myself. Help me get my eyes off of me and onto you! Give me wisdom and words that will allow others to see You and not me.

The Riot in Ephesus
Journal Entry   10 December 2014 (Snow Day)
Blog Entry   19 June 2019

Acts 19:23-41 - Paul in Ephesus
The Silversmiths in Ephesus were worried because they made their money selling statues of the goddess Artemis. The Ephesians had a long history of honouring Artemis as their god of fertility. They had statues of her everywhere and would have festivals to honour her with wild orgies.

Although Paul doesn't speak against her, only in favour of Jesus, the Silversmiths are worried their livelihood will be affected by Paul's teachings. They incite a riot to get rid of Paul and his companions but are ultimately unsuccessful.

The lesson I felt in my spirit from this passage was that we need to make decisions in life based on the right motives, which are *never* about making more money. God will take care of you financially if you make your decisions based on Biblical principles. Strive to serve God and not money! This is really helping me in my decision to cut back to working 4 days a week when I turn 53 in April and to retire for sure at 55. I believe God has a new chapter ready for me to write and many exciting things planned for me to do! Thank you, Lord! I praise you for what you have waiting for me to do!

Update - 19 June 2019

Kind of fun to read this note from almost five years ago when I was trying to make difficult decisions about working and considering how that would impact our financial situation. We had just finished putting two kids through post-secondary school and had paid for a wedding. We had an enormous mountain of debt at the time. However, I did indeed cut back to working only four days a week the next year and did retire at fifty-five. It made absolutely no sense financially, but we did it anyway. I felt certain this is what God was calling me to do. Guess what happened? Through a set of various circumstances, God more than provided for all our needs! We even have enough money now to send our youngest daughter to a private Christian school. Praise you, God, Jehovah Jireh, for Your immense blessings on our family and for Your Word, which is truth. When we choose to follow You, to listen and obey Your still small voice guiding and directing us, our lives are full of hope and promise.

"For my yoke is easy to bear, and the burden I give you is light." - Matt 11:30 NLT

Paul Says a Final Goodbye to the Ephesian Elders
Journal Entry   11 December 2014
Blog Entry   21 June 2019

Acts 20:16-38
Paul is leaving Ephesus, and everyone is sad because he knows he won't be back there and won't ever see them again. He knows that he must continue his journeys, and the Lord has made him aware that it won't be easy. Even though he knows that many difficult trials await him, it doesn't weaken his faith or affect his resolve to do what he knows is right, what God is calling him to do!

No matter the ups and downs of our lives, God is constant, the same, always good, never changing. Our faith and hope in Him should remain at the same commitment level no matter what our circumstances.

Paul Returns to Jerusalem
Journal Entry   12 December 2014
Blog Entry   24 June 2019

Acts 21 & 22
Paul goes to Jerusalem even though everyone warns him not to, and he knows he will be treated badly there. Paul knows he must go there to witness and testify to the Gospel message. He has to tell the truth to those who don't want to hear it, even if it means he has to die.

We are always called to tell our story of our experiences with Jesus so that others will learn of His presence and realness in the world. They need to hear our stories and know that it can be for them as well. They will soon also have a story to tell.

God was Doing Something New
Paul addresses the crowd of Jewish people. They want to kill him because he is allowing Gentiles to know about God and be part of His people. The first thing that hit me in reading this was that many times in Acts, people gang up to incite a riot. I also noticed this in Acts 17:1-15. It

seems one person can't take on a person of God alone, so they gather a lot of people to start a riot and really get the crowd going. The second thing that stood out for me in reading this passage was that they became enraged and wanted to kill Paul when they heard the word "Gentile". As soon as they heard that Paul was spreading God's word to the Gentiles, it set them off. They were all about separating themselves from others. That was the way it was in the Old Testament. God had instructed them to keep themselves separate as a people, and they just couldn't change that way of thinking. God was doing something new, but they couldn't accept that.

A Storm on the Way to Rome
Journal Entry   18 December 2014
Blog Entry   26 June 2019

Acts 27:13-26 - The Storm at Sea
In Acts 27, Paul is being transported to Rome as a prisoner due to the accusations made against him by the Jewish authorities. The journey is filled with delays, and Paul warns the crew that it is now too late in the season to continue sailing. However, the crew presses on. As Paul predicted, an enormous storm comes upon them, and it seems as if they won't survive. One night during the storm, an angel appears to Paul and assures him that he will make it to Rome, as will all the crew. As the Angel said, they all survived.

Fear Not
"Fear Not." At Lifecentre we are in a series called "Fear Not", and twice in Acts I have noticed that Angels have told Paul "Fear Not". Though Paul's journeys did not always turn out as planned and had many detours, God had a steady plan in it all for His glory on the earth.

Today I am hearing God call to me, "Fear Not. Stay close

to me, and I will guide you through every trial and every triumph, for they are all for My Glory!" Praise be to God, for He alone is HOLY! Amen.

Update - 26 June 2019

In the past couple of years, the Lord has been teaching me a new dimension of "Fear Not". I had a tendency to become worried about bad things that might happen, even though there was really no good reason to think they would. For example, when my son was a new driver, I would have visions or ideas in my mind about accidents that might happen on his way to school. Over the past year or so, I've felt the Lord teaching me that I need to capture these thoughts and toss them away. This negative thinking is simply an attack by the thief, the enemy of my soul, trying to steal my joy and destroy my peace. Now, when these thoughts rise up in my mind, I recognize them for what they are, lies of the enemy. I push those ridiculous thoughts out and lift any concern I have in prayer to God. It's pretty amazing how much joy and peace floods my mind when I choose not to let these negative thoughts take hold.

[10] The thief comes only to steal and kill and destroy; I have come that they may have life, and have it to the full. John 10:10 NIV

Paul as a Prisoner in Rome
Journal Entry   19 December 2014
Blog Entry   28 June 2019

Acts 28:11-31
Paul was brought to Rome to be tried and sentenced to death for preaching the Gospel message in Jerusalem. When he got to Rome, he was allowed to live by himself with a soldier to guard him. He ended up staying there for two years and continued to preach the Gospel message.

So, he was a prisoner, and was sent to Rome to be sentenced to death because he was preaching the Gospel, but when he got there, he used the opportunity to spread the message further. He was sometimes confined to his house but would receive visitors and teach them. He wrote Ephesians, Colossians, and Philippians, sometimes referred to as his prison letters, and Philemon, during this two-year house arrest. Paul had written, Romans, his letter to the church in Rome, three years before arriving there under arrest.

Planting Small Seeds Matters

Paul didn't even start up the church of believers in Rome. The church in Rome was started up by Jews who had travelled to Jerusalem for Passover and received the Holy Spirit during Pentecost, forty days after Jesus' death and resurrection. They returned to Rome to tell others the amazing things that had happened during the Passover that year. Look what's in Rome now, the Vatican!

For me, the lesson here is, never pass up an opportunity to reach others for Christ. It's your life's most important work, so don't give up. Even when you are rejected or persecuted or feel like you have failed. Don't give up trying! Even if you mess it up a lot, keep trying. Keep telling others about Jesus, about the impact your relationship with Him has had on your life. Tell others about who He is and what He has done for each and every one of us.

Update 28 June 2019

[15] *The brothers and sisters there had heard that we were coming, and they travelled as far as the Forum of Appius and the Three Taverns to meet us. At the sight of these people, Paul thanked God and was encouraged. Acts 28:15 NIV*

Can you imagine how Paul felt after all he'd been through? He was brought as a prisoner from Jerusalem, endured a shipwreck, and was finally arriving in Rome. As he arrives, he is greeted by a group of believers that he had never even met! On reading this passage this morning, I could feel the joy in my heart that he must have felt at that sight.

SUMMER

3

PAUL'S LETTER TO THE CHURCH IN ROME

Paul Longs to Visit and Share the Gospel with the Church in Rome
Journal Entry   22 December 2014
Blog Entry   1 July 2019

Chosen by God

In the beginning of Paul's letter to the Roman Believers, he talks about being chosen by God to be an apostle. I felt a revelation on reading this that I have also been chosen by God to belong to Jesus. I've been called into the family of God, and as a member of this family, I have a responsibility to reach others with His word. Please teach me and guide me, Holy Spirit. Help me to boldly and courageously speak to others about you. Help me reach those you would have me reach with your message. Make me bolder. Help me speak up and not be afraid!

⁶ And you also are among those Gentiles who are called to belong to Jesus Christ. ⁷ To all in Rome who are loved by God and called to be his holy people: Grace and peace to you from God our Father and from the Lord Jesus Christ. (Romans 1:6-7 NIV)

Prevented from Doing What is in Our Hearts

Romans 1:13 also stuck out to me today. Paul said he had wanted to do something but had been prevented from doing it. This brought to mind my yearly tithing. Tithing is something that I've felt convicted about for the past few years. It was hard to start tithing when it wasn't something we had built into our family budget. Since we always had just enough, and sometimes not quite enough, to pay our regular bills, it was quite a challenge to find room in our finances for tithing. I tried the best I could to tithe, and sometimes, I would fall a bit behind. I would keep track of how much I was behind and catch up when I had extra pay or unexpected money.

So I fully intended and wanted to catch up on our yearly tithing this year with our back pays and Dad's Christmas money. However, we unexpectedly got this huge bill to fix our son's car, almost equal to what I wanted to tithe. Unfortunately, I had to pay for the car repairs rather than tithing. I had recently been feeling guilty about that. On reading this passage in Romans, I realized that maybe I'm not meant to feel guilty about it as there is no condemnation in Christ! My heart was in the right place, but circumstances prevented me from being able to do it.

Speaking to Your Listeners

Finally, I was also struck today by the fact that when Paul was teaching the Good News, the Gospel, the message about what Jesus had done on the cross for mankind, that it was unknown. The idea of Christianity was a totally new concept for people at that time. In our world today, most people I interact with already have some knowledge, usually not totally accurate knowledge, but some knowledge of Jesus. I felt the Holy Spirit telling me that we need to teach the Gospel message differently in this time. We need to use a different approach than Paul did because we are reaching a different audience. It's not enough to just tell people Jesus died for their sins, they know that, but they don't understand it, or know how it can impact them before they die. They need to know how their lives can begin to change the moment they receive Jesus into their hearts. That eternal life, abundant life, starts at that point. It's not just about what happens after they die.

Trading God for Sin
Journal Entry   23 December 2014
Blog Entry   3 July 2019

Romans 1:18-32 is a very powerful and important message, particularly in today's culture, where every sin imaginable is not only tolerated in our society but even encouraged. This isn't something new but was also going on 2000 years ago when Paul wrote this letter. Paul tells the Romans the hard truth that rejection of God will lead to sinful lives. When we reject or fail to acknowledge God, He will give us over to foolish, sinful, and wicked desires.

^{23} And instead of worshiping the glorious, ever-living God, they worshiped idols made to look like mere people and birds and animals and reptiles. ^{24} So God abandoned them to do whatever shameful things their hearts desired. As a result, they did vile and degrading things with each other's bodies. ^{25} They traded the truth about God for a lie. (Romans 1:23-25 NLT)

Because they Abandoned God, He Abandoned them to Unnatural Sexual Relations

So, they worshiped and served the things God created instead of the Creator himself, who is worthy of eternal praise! Amen. ^{26} That is why God abandoned them to their shameful desires. Even the women turned against the natural way to have sex and instead indulged in sex with each other. ^{27} And the men, instead of having normal sexual relations with women, burned with lust for each other. Men did shameful things with other men, and as a result of this sin, they suffered within themselves the penalty they deserved. (Romans 1:25-27 NLT)

Since they Abandoned God, He Allowed their Lives to Become Full of Wickedness

²⁸ Since they thought it foolish to acknowledge God, he abandoned them to their foolish thinking and let them do things that should never be done. ²⁹ Their lives became full of every kind of wickedness, sin, greed, hate, envy, murder, quarrelling, deception, malicious behaviour, and gossip. ³⁰ They are backstabbers, haters of God, insolent, proud, and boastful. They invent new ways of sinning, and they disobey their parents. ³¹ They refuse to understand, break their promises, are heartless, and have no mercy. (Romans 1:28-31 NLT)

Gossip

I see this list of sinful behaviours in Romans 1:29 as the opposite of the Fruit of the Spirit. Finding "gossip" listed along with "hate, envy, and murder" is interesting. We may not have thought of gossip as such a vile thing, but we should be wary of its power in our lives and resist the temptation to engage in this behaviour.

The overall deeper meaning of this passage that I felt in my spirit was that when we choose to ignore God, we get ourselves into trouble. These sinful behaviours all go against what God intended for us and how God intended for us to live. We will all have to deal with desires in our lives that we must strive to control if we want to live the life God wants us to have, but God will help us if we give Him room to work in our lives.

Giving God Room to Work

Another important message in this part of Romans 1 for me was that God is not calling us to be superheroes of avoiding all temptation. He is calling us to acknowledge Him in our lives! He's calling us to put Him first, to honour Him, to give Him His rightful place as our creator, provider, and Saviour. The message for me is that when we put Him first, He will guide us and direct us. When we give Him His rightful place in our lives, He will stay with us and not abandon us to wrong behaviours and thinking. It is not about living the perfect life; it's about receiving His gift of grace, accepting it, and then listening to His still small voice directing us in our behaviours and decision making. When we refuse to give Him space in our lives, we won't be able to hear Him.

Jews & Gentiles
Journal Entry   24 December 2014 (Christmas Eve)
Blog Entry   5 July 2019

[28] For you are not a true Jew just because you were born of Jewish parents or because you have gone through the ceremony of circumcision. [29] No, a true Jew is one whose heart is right with God… (Romans 2:28-29 NLT)

From a spiritual perspective, I've always felt inferior to a Jewish person. After all, they are God's chosen people, the children of God, and I was born a mere Gentile. But this passage makes me feel that I am just as much a child of God as a person who has a Jewish heritage. If my heart has been changed by God to serve Him, I can confidently proclaim that I am a true member of God's family.

A Person with a Changed Heart Seeks Praise from God and not from People

…And true circumcision is not merely obeying the letter of the law; rather, it is a change of heart produced by the Spirit. And a person with a changed heart seeks praise from God, not from people. (Romans 2:29 NLT)

The Faith of Abraham
Journal Entry   30 December 2014
Blog Entry   10 July 2019

Even when there was no reason for hope Abraham kept hoping, believing that he would become the father of many nations (Romans 4:19 NLT)

Even after Abraham was 100 years old and Sarah was way past the age of bearing children, Abraham still had faith in God's promise. There was no logical reason to hope, but he kept hoping. God had promised him he would be the father of many nations, but even though it looked like this would never happen, he still had faith.

Faith is the Key
In Romans 4, Paul tries to help us understand the free gift of righteousness, that being right with God isn't about works (the things we do) or being right under the law, because it is impossible to be right under God's law! All we need is to have faith, believe in God, believe that He is always working for our good, and trust the leading of His Holy Spirit, even when things in our lives seem impossible.

God's Plan is Better than Mine
At this point in my life, I feel the Lord is calling me to eat right, exercise, lose some weight, and also begin working less in order to spend more time in Kingdom work. I also feel that He is calling me to spend more time with the kids. This seems contrary to what I should do because we have so much debt right now. We are currently over $100,000 in debt, not to mention $170,000 still owing on the mortgage. It makes absolutely no sense for me to cut back on work hours. I hear God calling, but I wonder how in the world we will be able to pay off all this debt. However, when I get worried about the money and think I can't go to four days a week and lose 20% of my pay, I hear God saying, "Fear Not". I know I need to trust that God knows better, that He knows the future, and somehow this debt will still get paid with me working less 0: Fear Not, have faith, trust Me.

Update - 19 October 2015

My Dad died less than a month after I wrote the entry above. While it wasn't a complete shock, as he hadn't been well for many years, death is never welcome, and is never well-enough prepared for. I was with him when he died, which was an incredible experience that I'll write about some other time. I did start working a four-day workweek that winter. Almost as soon as I started my reduced workweek, it turned out that my step-mom needed lots of help. This extra day off every week gave me room in the week to be able to take her for groceries.

Although this wasn't what I imagined I would be doing on my day off, I felt very sure that God was calling me to do this, and this turn of events was one of the reasons He needed me to cut back on my hours. Even though I wasn't able to see this coming back in December, God could. By September, my Step-Mom's health had declined to the point that she couldn't go grocery shopping with me anymore, but we had really enjoyed that summer doing groceries together and truly had fun together.

Financially, it got even worse for us during this time as I had less income, and on top of that, our son and his girlfriend moved in with us for a while. This made everything more expensive – more groceries and higher water bills. Even in the midst of all this, we were able to completely pay off one of our credit cards and almost catch up on our property tax payments. We are managing to continue paying down debt slowly, even though I'm working less and making less. I don't regret the decision to work less, and I know this is where God wants me to be. I do lose sight of Him from time to time, but then He'll suddenly come rushing back with confirmation that I'm on the right track which is so much fun!

Update - 10 July 2019

As I write this entry on the blog page today and see what God has brought us through these past four and a half years, I continue to be amazed by His faithfulness and His promises. Back in 2015, I trusted that God had a better plan in spite of what I could see with my human eyes, and in 2017 I did it again. I felt a very strong call from God to retire in 2017 even though we still owed most of that mountain of debt. My husband had retired six months prior, and my retirement was going to further cut back our income substantially. Again, this made no sense in the natural world, but I was quite certain this was what God was calling me to do, so I did it. A few months after I retired, we began regular volunteer work with our Church Foodbank and continued to tithe and slowly pay down our debts.

As of today, we are pretty much debt-free, except for about four years left to pay on the mortgage. Not only that, but we are able to afford to send our youngest child to a private Christian High School. We were also able to fix and/or replace many things that needed repair in our home.

None of this makes any sense in the natural financial world of buying and selling. It only makes sense in the spiritual world of sowing and reaping. God was calling us out to a different kind of life, a life of trusting Him more than we trusted ourselves. He called us to sow in His Kingdom. We heard and obeyed His call and trusted Him to help us with our needs. Wow, did He ever! I continue to be amazed by how God works in my life, and it is truly all about faith!

God's Law
Journal Entry   *3 January 2015*
Blog Entry   *12 July 2019*

[20] *God's law was given so that all people could see how sinful they*

were. But as people sinned more and more, God's wonderful grace became more abundant. [21] So just as sin ruled over all people and brought them to death, now God's wonderful grace rules instead, giving us right standing with God and resulting in eternal life through Jesus Christ our Lord. (Romans 5:20-21 NLT)

I love how my Life Application Study Bible explains these two verses:

"As a sinner, separated from God, you see his law from below, as an infinite ladder to be climbed to get to God. Perhaps you have repeatedly tried to climb it, only to fall to the ground every time you have advanced one or two rungs. Or perhaps the sheer height of the ladder seems so overwhelming that you have never even started up. In either case, what a relief you should feel to see Jesus offering with open arms to lift you above the ladder of the law, to take you directly to God! Once Jesus lifts you into God's presence, you are free to obey out of love, not necessity, and through God's power, not your own. You know that if you stumble, you will not fall back to the ground. Instead, you will be caught and held in Christ's loving arms."

What is the Law? Update - 12 July 2019

When I wrote this entry about the law back in 2015, I didn't fully understand what "The Law" meant. At that time, I thought God's Law was just the Ten Commandments that Moses had brought down from the mountain in Exodus 20. However, during a Bible class I was attending a few years later, my understanding of the law started to expand a little. Our teacher didn't go into what the whole law entailed, but some of his comments prompted me to believe that it was more than simply the Ten Commandments.

I did a bit of research today and found this on The Christian Broadcasting Network (CBN): *"So in the final analysis, God's law is that we should put God first in our lives. He wants us to function under Him as loving, obedient sons and daughters. We must listen to Him, obey Him, and be prepared to do His bidding, whatever it is."*

If putting God first in everything and always doing what He is calling me to do is *The Law*, then yes, I definitely fall short every day! I am so thankful that my God, my Creator, is so filled with grace and mercy for me that He continues to lift me up every time I fall. He knows that despite my best efforts, I will continue to fall and fail, but He has promised that He will continue to be there to catch me and bring me back into His loving embrace each and every time.

The Power of Sin Versus the Power of Christ
Journal Entry   5 January 2015
Blog Entry   17 July 2019

Sin isn't just a thing you do; it's a living, thriving environment and a way of life. There are only two camps you can belong to in life, the Sin Camp or the Christ Camp. The only way to get from the sin camp, to get away, the only way out, is to ask Jesus to save you. Once you've given your life to Jesus, the Sin Camp can't hold you anymore; you belong to the Christ Camp now. You might still fall back and do some of the things they do in the Sin (family) Camp; that's what you grew up knowing. It takes time to change habits and develop new patterns of living, but gradually you become more like the Christ family. When you fall, you are immediately forgiven by grace, and the Sin Camp can't get you back. The Sin Camp has no hold over you anymore. You have a new identity in the family of God.

We know that our old sinful selves were crucified with Christ so that sin might lose its power in our lives. We are no longer slaves to sin. ⁷ For when we died with Christ we were set free from the power of sin. (Romans 6:6-7 NLT)

The Relationship Between God's Law and Sin
Journal Entry   6 January 2015
Blog Entry   19 July 2019

But now we have been released from the law, for we died to it and are no longer captive to its power. Now we can serve God, not in the old way of obeying the letter of the law, but in the new way of living in the Spirit. (Romans 7:6 NLT)

The Law and its Hold Over Us
The law has no power over me after I have died with Christ by accepting Him as my Saviour. When I was baptized, it was a symbol of my death with Christ, the death of my former self. Now the law no longer applies to me in the same way because I have died to it by accepting Christ. The law no longer applies after the death to my life without Christ. So, I don't have to follow the law to please God. I am already fully pleasing to God because of Christ. But I do follow the law and do good works in the world, not because I am being judged by the law, but because I am now a partner with Christ in bringing God's glory to the world. God's glory is magnified in my obedience to the law.

God's Law Reveals Our Sin
7 Well then, am I suggesting that the law of God is sinful? Of course not! In fact, it was the law that showed me my sin. I would never have known that coveting is wrong if the law had not said, "You must not covet."8 But sin used this command to arouse all kinds of covetous desires within me! If there were no law, sin would not have that power. 9 At one time, I lived without understanding the law. But when I learned the command not to covet, for instance, the power

of sin came to life, 10 and I died. So, I discovered that the law's commands, which were supposed to bring life, brought spiritual death instead. 11 Sin took advantage of those commands and deceived me; it used the commands to kill me. (Romans 7:7-11 NLT)

If we didn't have God's laws, we would not know what was right or wrong. Therefore, no matter what we did, we could never be guilty of sin, or at least, we would never be able to feel that guilt and eventually repent. However, the law shows us what is right and wrong. Once we know something is wrong and choose to do it anyway, we experience spiritual death. We separate ourselves from God and are now under the spiritual power of the enemy. It's inevitable that we will sin, as we are human, and no one save Jesus is capable of living without committing at least one sin in their lifetime. God knew this, so He devised a way to save us from spiritual death. The way He saved us was by sending Jesus, the one with no sin, to take our sin on him and die on the cross. So, when Jesus died, He took on himself the punishment for all of the sins humanity would ever commit. We are released from spiritual death and made alive again in our relationship with God by accepting Christ's sacrifice for us and believing in this divine exchange.

Struggling with Sin
14 So the trouble is not with the law, for it is spiritual and good. The trouble is with me, for I am all too human, a slave to sin. 15 I don't really understand myself, for I want to do what is right, but I don't do it. Instead, I do what I hate. 16 But if I know that what I am doing is wrong, this shows that I agree that the law is good. 17 So I am not the one doing wrong; it is sin living in me that does it. (Romans 7:14-17 NLT)

Update - 19 July 2019

Wow, I found Romans 7 so helpful to me today in my

continued struggle to do the things I know I should do in this life. Thank you, Jesus, that you came to lift us above our struggles, to give us new hope and new life. Thank you for reminding me today that when I feel defeated and lost in my efforts to do right, I just need to look up to You. You will swoop me up out of that pit of struggle and despair. It's no surprise to You that I struggle. I am human and will always struggle with sinful ways, but that's why you came. To save me from myself and hopelessness.

Breaking Free from Legalistic Thinking
Journal Entry   12 January 2015
Blog Entry   22 July 2019

Personal Thoughts
Well, it's been about a week since I've written and read Your word in the morning. A lot happened last week. I was sick with a cold and stayed home for most of the week. Paris was attacked by terrorists using the name of Islam as their motivation, so I watched a lot of news last week. I'm really hoping we are reaching a turning point where the world will see these terrorists for what they are more clearly and will learn how to defend itself more vigorously from these people. I love what I am seeing with many faiths coming together in love and respect. I pray that God will guide us safely through this time in history.

Jesus Sets Us Completely Free from Sin
My bible reading today is Romans 7:4 to 25. It's great because Pastor J is also currently doing a series on sin, so I'm learning a lot about sin, very revealing. Something I learned in the service this week was that Jesus' death makes us truly, completely free of sin. We don't have to do any works at all and could break every commandment, and we would still be seen as righteous to God because the power of sin over us died with Jesus. So as Paul puts it, we don't have to worry about sin which makes it less of an

obstacle or stumbling block in our lives. We can go out and spend our time doing good things to glorify God.

Battling Sin and Personal Expectations
This feels like a shift for me from legalism. I think I was a little too legalistic before and had too many expectations of myself, my husband, kids, etc. I'm feeling a bit freer. Paul struggled with sin, just as we all do. It's a lifelong journey, and the battlefield is your life, fighting this out every day by everything you do.

Sweet Refuge Nestled in Jesus' Love for Us and Presence in Our Lives
There is a sweet refuge when we allow ourselves to see that even though we fall, we are still seen by God as His righteous children because of what Jesus did for us. We are God's children. His heirs, called by Him and made clean by Christ. We need to go out into the world every day led by His Holy Spirit to do His works with our heads held high despite our mistakes, imperfections, and inadequacies. We may be weak and vulnerable, but He is strong and will be strong for us! He will carry us through every trial and valley and celebrate with us on every mountaintop!

"So, my dear brothers and sisters, this is the point: You died to the power of the law when you died with Christ and now you are united with the one who has raised you from the dead. As a result, we can produce a harvest of good deeds for God!" (Romans 7:4 NLT)

I love Romans 7:4!

Living Under the Control of Our Sinful Nature or by the Holy Spirit
Journal Entry   13 January 2015
Blog Entry   26 July 2019

Those who are dominated by the sinful nature think about sinful things, but those who are controlled by the Holy Spirit think about things that please the Spirit. ⁶ So letting your sinful nature control your mind leads to death. But letting the Spirit control your mind leads to life and peace. ⁷ For the sinful nature is always hostile to God. It never did obey God's laws, and it never will. ⁸ That's why those who are still under the control of their sinful nature can never please God. (Romans 8:5-8 NLT)

Death or Life

What does Paul mean by "Death" in this passage? In the larger context, I believe he means spiritual, the kind that goes beyond this mortal, bodily experience. It means death to who you could have been in this life. You may still have a long physical life, but a life wasted on minor selfish pleasures instead of the life you could have lived contributing your gifts to God's Kingdom on earth. When you die, it will mean eternal separation from your creator.

On a more personal scale, "death" would refer to things that you lose out on because you choose to sin instead of doing what you know is the right thing to do. For example, if I overeat and neglect exercise, I will cause "death" to my full enjoyment of living. I will not be able to move as freely as I could have if I had taken better care of myself. Furthermore, I will constantly feel bad about being overweight. All these little personal battles add up to a life living in death instead of the abundance of life and peace.

Our Mind is the Battlefield

It is a battle of the mind. If we want to live our best life, we must fight to allow the Holy Spirit control over our minds instead of allowing the sinful nature to control our minds.

Update - 26 July 2019

This one simple truth is a key that unlocks everything we

need in life! However, the battle is never-ending while we are living and breathing on this earth. Unfortunately, we have to fight this fight in our minds every day. I keep waiting and hoping for the day when everything will be easy, the day I won't entertain a single sinful thought, but I think that day is unlikely to come, that this is a lifelong battle. Although, I think it does get easier as the Holy Spirit continues to transform us to look more like Jesus.

God's Powerful Love for Us
Journal Entry   14 January 2015
Blog Entry   29 July 2019

Wow! Romans 8 is packed with wisdom and encouragement for our lives. I need to remember to go to this Chapter and soak it in, particularly in times of discouragement or disappointment. This chapter reminds us of who we really are and how powerfully our God loves us!

Who We are and Our Future Hope
Verses 18 to 30 talk about the future glory when we will all be united – all the children of God with Jesus. We will have new bodies that will not decay and die. Sickness will become unimaginable. It's hard for us to imagine that, but it's wonderful to have that hope of the future always in front of us. So, no matter what happens in this life, we have that to look forward to. These verses also remind us of just who we are, that we are God's children. He chose us ahead of time, before we were even born, or knew who He was. He is continually calling out to us to live the lives full of purpose that He had prepared for us.

The Most Powerful and Unimaginable Love
In verses 31 to 39, Paul explains so well how nothing can separate us from the love of God, the love that God has for us. God is omniscient and omnipresent, all-knowing, and everywhere all at once, yet He still loves us completely

no matter where we are or what is happening in our lives. He continues to love us and be right there with us in every moment. No one can take that away from us.

The only person who can take God away from us is ourselves, if we choose not to believe in Him and not to accept Him into our lives. In our deepest, darkest moments in life, God is there with us, even if we don't know it. Even if we choose not to acknowledge his presence, it doesn't make any difference; He is still there. He is still reaching out to us with His powerful love, no matter what we do.

Always Imperfect but Saved by Grace
Journal Entry   18 January 2015
Blog Entry   31 July 2019

"For Christ has already accomplished the purpose for which the law was given." (Romans 10:4 NLT)

Following the Law Versus Faith in Jesus
I believe one of the main reasons God gave us the law was so that we would realize that it is impossible for us to be right with God without some other way than keeping all the rules the law gives us to live by. This other way is Jesus!

Before Jesus, they had to offer all those sacrifices because they always sinned. It was, and still is, impossible to perfectly keep the law. We should try to keep the law but know that when we fail, we are covered by the blood of Jesus. We shouldn't beat ourselves up about it but just try our best again. It's not a matter of being good or bad. It's a matter of faith, of trusting that Jesus has given His life so that we can make mistakes, fall short of the law's guidelines, and still be right in God's eyes.

Living by Faith - Day by Day
Dear Jesus, please help me stop trying to do things in my own strength! Teach me how to trust You, and lean on You, and know You will get it done for me. I'm trusting that if I do the things I hear You calling me to do in a given day that you will get the rest done for me, You will fill in the gaps I can't see. Please help me remember this plan and put this into practice in my life. Right now, I hear You calling me to eat better, exercise, and show love to others. Help me focus on those things and not waste time worrying about other things I don't get done. More of you, Lord, and less of me today!

[10] *For it is by believing in your heart that you are made right with God, and it is by openly declaring your faith that you are saved. (Romans 10:10 NLT)*

It's Not About Us
Journal Entry   20 January 2015
Blog Entry   2 August 2019

The Stumbling Block
The stumbling block is that we must depend on God and not ourselves. How do we do this? We call on God to help us in every situation and realize that only with His help can we truly succeed and proceed to the life He has planned for us to live!

Isaiah (again!) gives us the metaphor for pulling this together:

Careful! I've put a huge stone on the road to Mount Zion, a stone you can't get around.
But the stone is me! If you're looking for me, you'll find me on the way, not in the way. (Romans 9:33 MSG)

Update – 2 August 2019

Romans 9:6-32 is a hard read. It kicks our pride right in the teeth. I went through it a few times in a couple of different translations as I was having trouble understanding what it meant.

It's up to God, Not Us

We have to accept that God determines who will win and who will lose, who will have a hard heart, and who will be open to God. For instance, God used Pharaoh to show many others His power. Pharaoh was chosen beforehand, by God, to play this part, the part of the villain, who would lose his own son. Also, God chose Jacob to receive the blessing that should have gone to his older brother Esau. This was God's plan beforehand. There was nothing Jacob or Esau could have done to change this.

This is rather sobering and humbling news but an important lesson, particularly for prideful people. We must surrender our hopes and dreams to God and then accept whatever outcome He provides. We should do all we can to live our best life but then rest in the knowledge that the outcome is in God's hands, not ours.

This is actually somewhat comforting as it helps me let go of envy and jealousy. It also helps me let go of striving. If I truly believe that God is over everything, and my true provider, then I need to be thankful for what I've been given and not be jealous or envious of what others have. If I can truly accept that God has chosen to give that to them, and this to me, then I need to rest in that truth and not be frustrated or envious. If I feel envious or frustrated, then I am second-guessing God's decision.

Who are you, a mere human being, to argue with God? Should the thing that was created say to the one who created it, "Why have you made me like this?" [21] When a potter makes jars out of clay, doesn't he have a right to use the same lump of clay to make one jar for decoration and another to throw garbage into? (Romans 9:20-21 NLT)

I need to accept whatever lot in life God has for me, be it the flowerpot or the garbage can. This is a revolutionary concept for me! Although it hits me hard in my pride zone, it is helpful in providing me a vision of what full surrender is all about, what completely putting God first can look like.

God's Mercy and Love for Israel
Journal Entry   21 January 2015
Blog Entry   5 August 2019

In Romans 11, Paul tells the Jewish people that the purpose of the Gentiles knowing God through Christ, and receiving God's blessing, is to make the Jews jealous so they will also want to know God more and will seek Him more. Paul goes on to say that if the Jews reject Jesus and the Gentiles benefit from this, how much more will the world benefit when/if the Jews were to accept Jesus. They never achieve real freedom, real truth in this life, because they don't accept Jesus.

However, Paul also states that God will never abandon the Jewish people because He made them a promise, and He is a covenant-keeping God who never goes back on His promises.

[28] Many of the people of Israel are now enemies of the Good News, and this benefits you Gentiles. Yet they are still the people he loves because he chose their ancestors Abraham, Isaac, and Jacob. [29] For God's gifts and his call can never be withdrawn. (Romans 11:28-29 NLT)

Entering the Kingdom Like a Child
Journal Entry   22 January 2015
Blog Entry   7 August 2019

Little bit of a departure today from my regular reading schedule. The Lord laid some thoughts on my mind, so I took a break from Romans today.

Living in A Beautiful Place of Peace and Contentment
In my prayer time today, I talked to God about wanting to always be living in that beautiful feeling of contentment and innocence. I've found that when I purposefully take time out to devote to God, particularly in the morning, then later on during my day, I get these little bits of time when I just feel this inexplicable sense of peace and contentment. The only thing I can equate it to is remembering how it felt to be a child, a small child, walking to school in complete happiness with no responsibilities. This morning I asked God for more of this beautiful sense of His presence and peacefulness in my life, and in my day, because it's refreshing to be in this place in your mind and soul. While I was pondering this, God reminded me of the scripture about becoming like a child to enter the Kingdom of Heaven. Then I realized that this freedom I remember as a child is what He was talking about.

Who are You Depending On?
When you are a small child, you are completely dependent on your parent for everything. You have no cares or worries because you are not capable of taking care of yourself, and you have learned that your parent will take care of all your needs. Likewise, to experience this place of peace in your life as an adult, you need to become totally dependent on God and trust Him for everything. I mean, you are, of course, totally dependent on God, whether you realize it or not, but you need to grasp that mentally and live it out. I believe we lose that sense of peace in our lives as we grow from being a small child dependent on our parents and start to depend on ourselves. The good news

is we can get it back if we can become like that child again by knowing that we are fully dependent and fully cared for by God.

[16] Then Jesus called for the children and said to the disciples, "Let the children come to me. Don't stop them! For the Kingdom of God belongs to those who are like these children. [17] I tell you the truth, anyone who doesn't receive the Kingdom of God like a child will never enter it." (Luke 18:16-17 NLT)

More of You, God, and Less of Me
Journal Entry   26 January 2015
Blog Entry   9 August 2019

More of You and Less of Me
This has been a theme that started rolling through my soul beginning a week ago Sunday. During Sunday worship two weeks ago, this thought, *more of You and less of me,* popped into my thinking.

For everything comes from Him, exists by His power, and is intended for His glory. All glory be to Him forever. Amen. (Last verse of Romans 11, Romans 11:36 NLT)

All last week I had the most amazing peace-filled week because I kept remembering to ask You for more of You and less of me. It was truly amazing, I was able to handle situations that I wouldn't have handled well perhaps, but You helped me to handle them lovingly and perfectly. Dad went home to be with You very early Saturday morning while I was with him. I believe You ordained me to be the one there for that special moment, and I thank You for that privilege. As I enter this week and open Your word, I pray that this week there will be even more of You and less of me! Please help me be a blessing to everyone I can, and please help me to stir hearts for You.

I feel that I went deeper in my relationship with You this past week, and I thank You for the honour of being able to see some of You I hadn't seen before. I pray that You will continue to reveal more of Your beauty to me as I commit to continue pressing close to know You more!

Romans 12 – Personal Responsibilities

Wow, this is an awesome chapter! So direct! I need to remember this one that sums up how we should live our lives.

Don't copy the behaviour and customs of this world, but let God transform you into a new person by changing the way you think. Then you will learn to know God's will for you, which is good and pleasing and perfect. (Romans 12:2 NLT)

Update – 9 August 2019

I love the way Paul teaches us that it is all about God, all about Him, and His Glory, in chapter 11. Then right away, in chapter 12, he gives us instructions on how we should live. The order is perfect, as I believe that until we get to that place of surrender, of really giving God all authority over our lives, we will have a hard time following the instructions in chapter 12.

Don't just pretend to love others. Really love them. Hate what is wrong. Hold tightly to what is good. [10] Love each other with genuine affection, and take delight in honouring each other. [11] Never be lazy, but work hard and serve the Lord enthusiastically. [12] Rejoice in our confident hope. Be patient in trouble, and keep on praying. [13] When God's people are in need, be ready to help them. Always be eager to practice hospitality. [14] Bless those who persecute you. Don't curse them; pray that God will bless them. [15] Be happy with those who are happy, and weep with those who weep. [16] Live in harmony with each other. Don't be too proud to enjoy the company of ordinary people. And don't think you know it all! [17] Never pay back evil with more evil. Do things in such a way that everyone can see you are

honourable. ⁱ⁸ Do all that you can to live in peace with everyone.
¹⁹ Dear friends, never take revenge... (Romans 12:9-19 NLT)

Respect for Authority
Journal Entry   27 January 2015
Blog Entry   12 August 2019

In Romans 13:1-7, Paul gives us instructions regarding respect for authority and submitting to governing authorities. He states that the authorities are in these positions because they have been placed there by God. If we rebel against them, we are rebelling against what God has instituted, and we will be punished. He goes on to say that if we do what is right, we will have no reason to fear authorities.

Update – 12 August 2019

Back in 2015 when I wrote this entry, I didn't expand on it at all and, that's a bit unusual for me. I think it was due to the fact that my dad had just died a few days before this, and I was busy getting ready for his visitation and funeral. I was going through a lot of difficult emotions and tensions in myself and with my siblings. To be honest, I've always struggled a bit with authority, and I realized today that the root of this may actually relate to my dad as an authority figure in my life.

Imperfect Leaders in an Imperfect World
In a perfect world, I can completely accept Paul's instructions. The authority figures would act justly and appropriately according to God's laws, and everything would be wonderful. However, I find this passage near impossible to live out in today's world. It seems that governments and politicians are so corrupt and make decisions that hurt people. It is difficult to imagine that God would want us to respect these authorities and accept

their reprehensible treatment of others.

I guess it comes down to the fact that we live in a broken world filled with broken people. For instance, in my own family, my dad made mistakes that caused marriage break up and pain to my mom and pain in my life. Although I had looked up to him as my father, it was difficult to accept him as the authority figure when he did things that brought us pain and were inconsistent with the way a good father should act. However, he always did provide for us and gave us good advice. It seems to me that many politicians are like this as well; they do some things well, other things not so well.

I think we also need to remember that Paul wrote these instructions in a time when the governments weren't exactly perfect either! The rulers were throwing people in jail and killing them for being Christians. Yet, Paul still instructs us to respect these authorities.

The Life Application Study Bible lists three positions Christians take when it comes to the government or state:

1. The state is so corrupt that they have decided to have nothing to do with it. They don't vote, nor do they work for the government.
2. The state has authority over some things, and the church has authority over other things. They can be loyal to both as long as the spheres of authority don't mix.
3. Christians have a responsibility to make the state better. They can do this by voting for Christian or highly principled leaders. They also do this by serving as a good influence in society

I think position number three is the one I take. I do my best to respect authority and try to do my part to make society better. However, when authority figures go against what I know God's word is clear about, I will not blindly follow the authority and do things contrary to God's laws.

The Danger of Criticism
Journal Entry   28 January 2015
Blog Entry   14 August 2019

Let the Lord judge whether they are right or wrong, and with the Lord's help they will do right. Romans 14:4 (NLT)

Update – 14 August 2019

I had written an entry on January 28, 2015, but it was very personal in nature and probably not helpful to share with others. However, it was so interesting that this scripture came up right at the same time that I was having a personal disagreement with some family members. It was the morning after my Dad's wake, and we were getting his eulogy ready for the funeral. There was a difference of opinion on what we should say about Dad's life. Sometimes things can look so wrong to one person yet right to another.

Encourage, Don't Discourage

I think the essence of what Paul is teaching us here is that we should not discourage each other by judging or criticizing their commitment to God. Obviously, if someone is completely off track and doing things contrary to scripture, we may need to gently point that out to them. However, if they are doing their best to serve God in the way they believe is right, we should not criticize them or tell them that our own way is better. It's not up to us to judge who is right. That's God's job.

In Paul's time the Jewish Christians would have been following the customs of only eating certain foods "approved by God" while the Gentiles would not have been following those same rules. I believe what Paul is trying to say here is that the Gentiles were not devalued in God's eyes simply because they were eating certain foods that the Jewish people did not. On the other hand, Paul also says that if eating something is going to negatively impact your fellow believer, then don't eat, or at least don't eat it in front of them.

I know and am convinced on the authority of the Lord Jesus that no food, in and of itself, is wrong to eat. But if someone believes it is wrong, then for that person it is wrong. [15] And if another believer is distressed by what you eat, you are not acting in love if you eat it. Don't let your eating ruin someone for whom Christ died. Romans 14:14-15 (NLT)

The bottom line for me is to always do our best to build one another up in faith and never tear each other down. Always encourage; never discourage.

4
PAUL'S 1ST LETTER TO THE CHURCH IN CORINTH

Staying Strong in Faith Within a Sinful Culture
Journal Entry   29 January 2015
Blog Entry   16 August 2019

My Study Bible's introduction to Paul's letters to the Corinthians tells us that the Christians in Corinth were having trouble staying strong within the culture. They were struggling against their environment, which was full of corruption and every conceivable sin.

The Church in Corinth

Corinth was a busy Seaport, a major cosmopolitan city, a trade centre. It was filled with idolatry and immorality. Paul established the Church in Corinth on his second missionary journey. In AD 55, Paul wrote four letters to the Corinthians. Two were lost. 1st Corinthians was actually his second letter, and 2nd Corinthians was his fourth. The Corinthians were struggling. They were a weak church, being undermined by immorality and spiritual immaturity. Paul wrote strong, clear letters to them to try and help them overcome some of the hard issues they were struggling with. After the first three letters, some of the believers responded, but others did not, and instead questioned Paul's authority and motives. This is the pretext for 2nd Corinthians.

The Wisdom of the World is Foolishness

So where does this leave the philosophers, the scholars, and the world's brilliant debaters? God has made the wisdom of this world look foolish. Since God in his wisdom saw to it that the world would never know him through human wisdom, he has used our foolish preaching to save those who believe. (1st Corinthians 1:20-21 NLT)

The wisdom of the world, the ways of the world, are foolishness in light of God's wisdom, and the *only* way we can receive God's wisdom is through *faith* in Christ. We don't receive God's wisdom through traditional man-made educational systems, but *purely* through faith in Jesus. This doesn't mean we shouldn't attend school or other educational institutions. We should most definitely use all the talents and abilities God has blessed us with! However, that type of learning will not help us receive the wisdom we can receive from God. Paul reflects that very few of those whom God had called to Himself were wise, or powerful, or wealthy, in the world's eyes, but they received God's wisdom and the guidance of His Holy Spirit, through faith in Him. The most important thing any of us can do in life is to have faith in God and faith in Jesus. It's so contrary to our world culture that says you have to *do* something to *get* something. In God's economy, you simply have to believe.

God wanted to make Himself available to everyone. Jesus' sacrifice on the Cross made Salvation, Eternal Life, and a Life guided by the wisdom of the Holy Spirit available to everyone! It's not limited to just smart, rich, and powerful people, but all have access to it.

[24] But to those called by God to salvation, both Jews and Gentiles, Christ is the power of God and the wisdom of God. [25] This foolish plan of God is wiser than the wisest of human plans, and God's weakness is stronger than the greatest of human strength. (1st Corinthians 1:24-25 NLT)

Quarrelling and Our Sinful Nature
Journal Entry   31 January 2015
Blog Entry   19 August 2019

Off today. Still on bereavement leave. Got up to pray and was right on time for Joyce Meyer's TV program. The show was about "Letting God Fight Your Battles". It felt like I was meant to see it because of the difficulties I'm going through with my siblings since Dad died. I'm feeling that there is a division between us. Joyce advises that I should pray about it, ask God to help me know what to do about this, and to have an attitude of forgiveness.

Quarrelling in Corinth
Paul tells the church in Corinth that they weren't ready to receive strong spiritual teaching because they were still babies in the Spirit. Paul says that he had to teach them "with milk", not with more powerful ways, as they weren't ready. He tells them that they still aren't ready for more powerful teaching because they are still giving in to their sinful natures. He can tell this because of the arguments they are having and the fact that they are quarrelling. When people are quarrelling, it shows that they are not fully living in the Spirit.

[2] I had to feed you with milk, not with solid food, because you weren't ready for anything stronger. And you still aren't ready, [3] for you are still controlled by your sinful nature. You are jealous of one another and quarrel with each other. Doesn't that prove you are controlled by your sinful nature? Aren't you living like people of the world? (1st Corinthians 3:2-3 NLT)

Quarrelling in my Family
This helps me and speaks to me about the powerful weight I keep feeling fall over me since Dad's death a few days ago. We are having disagreements regarding his will and how to care for his widow. I've come to see that all that is going on is just a huge display of everyone's sinful natures. If we were all mature in God's Spirit we could sit down calmly and discuss the various options, but too many of us are being controlled by our sinful nature.

Thank you, Holy Spirit, for showing me this today and

help me to hear your voice above the noise and to operate in the Spirit throughout this time of testing. Whenever I begin to fall into my sinful nature, please pull me back-up out of that pit! Father, please help me let my anger go, and the angry feelings I have toward my siblings. Please help me to rid myself of all unforgiveness I am holding onto against anyone. I know that I can't fully serve you if I am clouded by unforgiveness. I want to be so full of You, and hearing from You, that I won't be able to see the old me anymore!

I hear You telling me: Trouble will come, but it's what you do with the trouble that matters. You can't stop trouble from coming. That's why I came – to help you through it all.

I have told you these things, so that in me you may have peace. In this world you will have trouble. But take heart! I have overcome the world. (John 16:33 NIV)

It's God that Grows the Seed
Journal Entry   **3 February 2015**
Blog Entry   **21 August 2019**

So, neither the one who plants nor the one who waters is anything, but only God, who makes things grow. (1ˢᵗ Corinthians 3:7 NLT)

I pray, God, that you will grow the seed that has been planted and watered in my sister. It's very hard to see where you are in her these days, but I pray that you will save her from your enemies, renew her mind, and draw her close to yourself. It's hard for me to write this as I am very angry with her right now. I feel she is making many wrong decisions, but I know that you can redeem this situation. Please grow in my sister and brother God.

Update – 21 August 2019

I was going through such a difficult time with my siblings when I wrote the entry above that I missed the bigger message in the passage. Interesting how our emotions can make us blind to greater truths. In this case, I was so hurt that I had tunnel vision, and the passage was only speaking to me about my personal situation at the time.

Who's in Charge?

In this part of his letter to the church in Corinth, Paul addresses division in the church. The Church in Corinth was divided, as some of the members said they were following Apollos' teachings, while some were following Paul's teachings. There were arguments about whose way was better. In this passage, Paul tries to set them straight, explaining that neither Paul nor Apollos are important; what's important is that you are following God's leading.

I think we do the same thing here in 2019 when we cling to one preacher or another, or one church or another as the *right* one. These are just the messengers, the ones scattering and watering the seeds. God is the only one who grows the seed in us. We should guard ourselves against getting caught up in certain leaders or churches and remember that God is over it all. God is the ultimate source of our growth in the Kingdom.

What God Makes Available to Us
Journal Entry   4 February 2015
Blog Entry   23 August 2019

Don't you realize that all of you together are the temple of God and that the Spirit of God lives in you. (1ˢᵗ Corinthians 3:16 NLT)

I absolutely love this truth! The church on earth is not a building or an organization. The church that God is building on the earth is comprised of the Holy Spirit, who was released after Jesus ascension back to Heaven, living and moving in the lives of every person who willingly receives Jesus into their heart.

Stop deceiving yourselves if you think you are wise by the world's standards, you need to become a fool to become truly wise. For the wisdom of this world is foolishness to God.
(1st Corinthians 3:18-19 NLT)

This helps me remember that God gives us everything we have. God, working through the Holy Spirit, gives us every little bit of wisdom or intelligence we have. The human intelligence He allows us each to have is tiny compared to the vastness of wisdom He makes available to us if we choose to draw close to Him! Thank you, God, for drawing me to yourself so I can really learn, and learn what is true and good and right.

Only God Knows Our Deepest Motives
***Journal Entry**   5 February 2015*
***Blog Entry**   28 August 2019*

Therefore, do not pronounce judgment before the time, before the Lord comes, who will bring to light the things now hidden in darkness and will disclose the purposes of the heart. Then each one will receive his commendation from God. (1st Corinthians 4:5 ESV)

My lesson lately is that we shouldn't judge others because we don't know the other person's motives. We don't know their hearts. An example of this is playing out in my life now with the issues that are going on with my Dad's estate. There is discord among family members, and my step-mother's relatives. Some family members are angry with me for not agreeing to see things their way. The reason they are angry is that they are assuming certain motives for other people's actions.

The way I see it is that we cannot know the hearts of

others. Only God knows that. When our motivation is to truly serve God and to follow His lead, our lives will be filled to overflowing with joy. When we operate in our sinful nature, we become dissatisfied, argumentative, and even physically ugly. There's a heaviness that follows us, and surrounds us, and is plain to see for everyone we meet. We can't see it in ourselves, but others can.

This doesn't mean that we should let people cheat or hurt us, but if our motivation is to truly serve God, then we need to choose the path that leads others to God. For me, this means we should be showing the fruits of the Spirit; *love, joy, peace, patience, kindness, goodness, faithfulness, gentleness, and self-control* in all situations, not just when it's easy. Since bickering, anger, and hatefulness are not fruit that flows out from the Holy Spirit I need to choose not to go there.

My Body is the Temple of the Holy Spirit
Journal Entry 6 February 2015
Blog Entry 30 August 2019

I was worrying and wondering about the situation with my sisters and brother and my relationship with them in my prayer time today. God told me to get my eyes off myself! Focus on serving others rather than letting that cloud overtake you. (drew a little cloud in my notebook :0)

Or do you not know that your body is a temple of the Holy Spirit within you, whom you have from God? You are not your own, [20] for you were bought with a price. So glorify God in your body. (1st Corinthians 6:19-20)

This passage tells me that my body is the temple of the Holy Spirit, that this body was bought at a great price, and it is my duty and responsibility to take good care of it. Dear Lord, help me get back on track with dieting and exercising! Remind me when I'm tempted to overeat and not exercise that I must honour and glorify you! That it's not about me, it's about You and Your glory.

Don't you realize that your bodies are actually parts of Christ? (1 Corinthians 6:15 NLT)

God paid a high price for you so don't be enslaved by the world. Remember who you are in Christ! (1 Corinthians 7:23 NLT)

In 1st Corinthians 7, Paul talks about marriage and singleness. For some people, it's best to serve the Lord as a single person. For others, it's best to marry. But once you marry, you have more earthly responsibilities and have less time to spend with God and to serve God. Even though being married caused me more responsibilities, I'm glad we were married because now there are four more people alive to serve God.

Your Influence on Others
Journal Entry   9 February 2015
Blog Entry   2 September 2019

1st Corinthians chapter 8 is about Christian freedom. It focuses on whether or not Christians should eat food that was offered to idols. Paul says that it makes no difference in your walk with God or your salvation if you eat it because you know that the idols aren't gods anyway. As a Christian, you know there is only one true God.

However, he points out that if you do eat food that has been offered to an idol in the presence of another person, who is weaker in faith and understanding, they might lose their faith or somehow stumble in their journey toward a greater closeness with God. If they respect you as a solid Christian and see you doing this, they might think that you believe idols should be worshiped. This could confuse them and set them back in their journey of faith.

Therefore, even though it makes no difference to do these things that seem to go against the law, it's good not to do them if it makes others fall. You need to be aware of your influence on others and try to behave in a way that will build them up in their relationship with Jesus, not confuse them or set them back.

^{8} Food will not commend us to God. We are no worse off if we do not eat, and no better off if we do. ^{9} But take care that this right of yours does not somehow become a stumbling block to the weak.
(1st Corinthians 8:8-9 ESV)

Paul's Mission
Journal Entry   10 February 2015
Blog Entry   4 September 2019

^{14} In the same way, the Lord ordered that those who preach the Good News should be supported by those who benefit from it. ^{15} Yet I have never used any of these rights. And I am not writing this to suggest that I want to start now. In fact, I would rather die than lose my right to boast about preaching without charge.
(1st Corinthians 9:14-15 NLT)

Paul gives up his right to receive payment for his work as an apostle. He knows that Jesus gave him this job to preach the Good News to the world, and he has to do everything he can to save as many people as possible. He can't accept payment as one would normally be paid for their work because he's not doing it on his own initiative. It's a sacred contract that he and God have both signed. He never asks for payment, but instead relies on God to provide for all his needs.

^{17} If I were doing this on my own initiative, I would deserve payment. But I have no choice, for God has given me this sacred trust. ^{18} What then is my pay? It is the opportunity to preach the Good News without charging anyone. That's why I never demand my rights when

I preach the Good News. (1ˢᵗ Corinthians 9:17-18 NLT)

Paul also conforms himself as much as possible to whomever he is with in order to save them. His one goal is to preach the gospel and save as many people as he can. That goal is always front and centre in his mind, and all his choices are made in light of that mission. It is never about him or his own needs or desires, but always about spreading the Gospel message.

²² When I am with those who are weak, I share their weakness, for I want to bring the weak to Christ. Yes, I try to find common ground with everyone, doing everything I can to save some. ²³ I do everything to spread the Good News and share in its blessings.
(1ˢᵗ Corinthians 9:22-23 NLT)

Dealing With Temptation
Journal Entry   **11 February 2015**
Blog Entry   **7 September 2019**

¹³ The temptations in your life are no different from what others experience. And God is faithful. He will not allow the temptation to be more than you can stand. When you are tempted, he will show you a way out so that you can endure. (1ˢᵗ Corinthians 10:13 NLT)

²³ You say, "I am allowed to do anything" but not everything is good for you. You say, "I am allowed to do anything"—but not everything is beneficial. ²⁴ Don't be concerned for your own good but for the good of others. (1ˢᵗ Corinthians 10:23 NLT)

³³ I, too, try to please everyone in everything I do. I don't just do what is best for me; I do what is best for others so that many may be saved.
(1ˢᵗ Corinthians 10:33 NLT)

Behave in a way that will bring others to Christ. It is difficult to control your sinful nature, and you cannot do it on your own, so don't forget to ask God for help each and every morning!

Order in Humanity
Journal Entry   12 February 2015
Blog Entry   9 September 2019

In the first part of 1st Corinthians 11, Paul talks about order in humanity. He states that the head of every man is Christ, and the head of every woman is man, as the head of Christ is God. By head, he doesn't infer any kind of inferiority. We are all created equal, but there must be order to prevent chaos. Submission does not equal inferiority. It instead suggests mutual commitment and cooperation! You choose to submit to prevent chaos and disorder. God has provided a hierarchy to follow – God – Christ – man – woman. Christ is not inferior to God, just as woman is not inferior to man.

³ But there is one thing I want you to know: The head of every man is Christ, the head of woman is man, and the head of Christ is God. (1st Corinthians 11:3 NLT)

Spiritual Gifts and the One Body of Christ
Journal Entry   15 February 2015
Blog Entry   11 September 2019

In 1st Corinthians chapter 12, Paul explains that though we are all given different gifts, it is one Spirit that gives them. This was at the time, in opposition to the pagan way of thinking, that there were various gods for various things. Paul tells us there is only one Spirit, but He gives various gifts.

Comparing the Body of Christ, the Church on Earth, to the Human Body
Paul compares the spiritual gifts God gives each of us to parts of the human body. He tells us that as the church, we are all important parts that make up the body of the

church. Each part needs to play its role for it to all work together harmoniously. The parts of the body with less dignity must be more clothed and better protected, but each part is equally important. Each believer makes up the body of Christ on the earth, which is the Church. God gives each of us abilities and gifts to serve others and edify the church. We are called to be good stewards of the gifts God gives us. Just as all the parts of our human body work together for one purpose, and each has its own part to play, so each of us must work together as interwoven parts of the body of Christ on the earth. None is more important than another, and all are needed to do their part in the accomplishment of the common goal.

Every Part is Important
If the human body was all ears, then how would it see? If the Church was all healers, then who would preach? If all preachers, then who would organize? Every part is equally important for the church to work as effectively as possible. I feel that God is telling me to just do my part and not to try to do everyone else's part! The yoke is easy if you just focus on your own part :0

The Love Chapter
Journal Entry   17 February 2015
Blog Entry   13 September 2019

1 Corinthians 13 is often referred to as "the Love Chapter". Parts of this chapter are regularly read at wedding ceremonies. Paul gives the definition of love and tells us that love is more important than anything else. That even if we had all knowledge and wisdom, if we knew as much as God but didn't have love, it would all be worthless.

[4] Love is patient and kind. Love is not jealous or boastful or proud [5] or rude. It does not demand its own way. It is not irritable,

and it keeps no record of being wronged. ⁶ It does not rejoice about injustice but rejoices whenever the truth wins out. ⁷ Love never gives up, never loses faith, is always hopeful, and endures through every circumstance. (1ˢᵗ Corinthians 13:4-7 NLT)

The chapter is short, but also tells us that for now, in this life, we see things as if through a veil or clouded mirror, but eventually, we will see clearly. It also says that some things will pass away but not faith, hope, and love. They will endure forever, with love being the most important! Amen.

Spiritual Gifts of Tongues and Prophecy
Journal Entry   23 February 2015
Blog Entry   16 September 2019

Paul teaches in 1ˢᵗ Corinthians 14:1-25 that it is good to have the gifts of tongues and the gifts of prophecy. He continues that the gift of tongues strengthens self, whereas the gift of prophecy strengthens others.

Gift of Tongues
Paul says that it's great to have the gift of tongues, but also that unless there is someone with the gift to interpret what is said in tongues, then this gift is more of a personal gift for self-edification than a gift for the community of believers.

Paul makes the point that it is important to strengthen others, the whole Church, and if you speak in tongues (a private prayer language only understood by your spirit and God) publicly, then others won't understand you. The private prayer language can be a wonderful uplifting exchange between you and God, but it won't help others at all. On the contrary, it may cause confusion and push others away.

I see another meaning in this as well, that if you don't speak the culture's language when telling them about Jesus, they will not understand you. If your testimony is all in *churchspeak*, others outside the church might not understand what you're trying to tell them. You could both be speaking English, but if you don't speak to them in the cultural norms they understand, then they still might not get it. Back in Chapter 10, Paul also talked about adjusting yourself to the culture if necessary, to spread the good news. Not so much that you need to fall into the sin of the culture around you, but that you sometimes need to adapt yourself to others so that they can hear and really understand the message you are bringing to them.

Gift of Prophecy

The gift of prophecy benefits the entire community of believers as everyone, those inside and outside the church, are able to understand what the speaker is saying.

The Corinthians had some disorder in the church and in their worship. Paul wrote to them to offer some clarity and direction regarding the gifts of tongues and prophecy because some people were using their gifts inappropriately, which was causing others to fall. The Lord wants us to always be building up the community of believers. It is good to build personal spiritual strength privately but not to boast about your gifts publicly. Only use your gifts publicly if it builds the Church up.

Order in Worship
Journal Entry   4 March 2015
Blog Entry   18 September 2019

Paul continues his guidance in 1st Corinthians 14:26-39 with regard to building the Church community up by talking about order in worship. Worship among the Church in Corinth had become disorderly, so much so, that it was no longer building up the body of believers. Paul gives them instructions so that they can restore a sense of order during worship.

Rules for Women in Worship

Some of the rules Paul offers to the Corinthians require women to be submissive to men and not speak out in worship. This could be interpreted to say that women are inferior, have nothing valuable to offer, and should never speak in worship. However, that would be a wrong interpretation, one that disregards the context. Due to the mix of cultures in Corinth at that time, it made sense for Paul to establish this rule to help restore order, whereas this directive would not be required in our church today.

Submission Does not Equal Inferiority

It should also be noted that submission does not equal inferiority. Rather, submission allows for order. Jesus submitted Himself to God, but He was not less than God. He was equal to God, but submitted to allow for order. Similarly, the Bible directs that women should submit to their husbands. We all have unique strengths and gifts, but in order to use those gifts effectively in community and in families, there must be some form of order. Order requires submission from some and leadership from others.

Rules versus Freedom of the Holy Spirit to Move

It should also be noted that the Holy Spirit must be free to move in worship. Worship should not become so rigid and full of process and rules that there is no freedom of the Spirit or allowance for creativity. God is the creator of the universe; creativity is important and should be allowed to flow as long as the community is built up.

The Resurrection of the Dead
Journal Entry   *5 March 2015*
Blog Entry   *21 September 2019*

Paul exhorts that we must believe in the resurrection of the dead and in Christ's resurrection, or there is no point to our faith. Just as death came into the world through one man Adam, the resurrection of the dead has begun through another man, Jesus!

Just as everyone dies because we all belong to Adam, all who belong to Jesus are given life. (1st Corinthians 15:21NLT)

Christ's Return to Earth

This chapter offers insight into the resurrection of the dead who have died believing in Christ. Paul asserts that at some point, Christ will come back to earth in bodily form, and all of those who died believing in Him will be resurrected and will join Him. Christ will defeat every spec of evil on the earth, with the last evil enemy to be destroyed being death itself. Then Christ will turn the Kingdom over to God.

Physical Bodies versus Spiritual Bodies

Paul explains that our physical bodies die, but our spiritual bodies, our resurrected bodies, will not be the same as our physical bodies. Paul compares our physical bodies to seeds that are put in the ground and are buried, and then a plant, something completely different, but that came from the dead seed, grows.

"Our bodies are buried in brokenness but they will be raised in glory" (1st Corinthians 15:43 NLT)

"Adam the first man came from the dust of the earth, while Christ the second man came from heaven".
(1st Corinthians 15:47 NLT)

Earthly people are like the earthly man, and heavenly people are like the heavenly man. Our physical bodies cannot inherit the Kingdom of God.

"These dying bodies cannot inherit what will last forever."
(1st Corinthians 15:50 NLT)

We need eternal heavenly bodies to enjoy eternal life. But not all will die. Those who are alive when the last trumpet sounds will be transformed in the blink of an eye. In other words, all those believers who are still alive in their earthly bodies here on earth when Christ comes back will be immediately transformed into their heavenly bodies.

Update - 21 September 2019

While going over 1st Corinthians 15:39-41 in the Message version of the Bible, I was struck by the idea that our heavenly bodies will not all be the same. Just as there is immense variety in our earthly bodies, there will be even more diversity in our heavenly bodies. Don't you find that fascinating?

$^{39-41}$ You will notice that the variety of bodies is stunning. Just as there are different kinds of seeds, there are different kinds of bodies—humans, animals, birds, fish—each unprecedented in its form. You get a hint at the diversity of resurrection glory by looking at the diversity of bodies not only on earth but in the skies—sun, moon, stars—all these varieties of beauty and brightness. And we're only looking at pre-resurrection "seeds"—who can imagine what the resurrection "plants" will be like!
(1 Corinthians 15:39-41MSG)

Respecting Our Church Youth
Journal Entry   7 March 2015
Blog Entry   23 September 2019

^{10} *When Timothy comes, don't intimidate him. He is doing the Lord's work, just as I am.* ^{11} *Don't let anyone treat him with*

contempt. Send him on his way with your blessing when he returns to me. I expect him to come with the other believers.
(1st Corinthians 16:10-13 NLT)

In our church, we often talk about the next generation building the Church from the place our generation left it. We don't want our kids to start at ground zero, but to continue from the "floor" we were able to get to. If you think about Christ's Church on earth as a building, then perhaps our generation was able to build twenty floors. We want our kids to start at floor twenty and keep going. We are raising up our youth to take over where we leave off, not to start all over again. However, we are building together while both our generations are here on earth, and we need to respect each other and what the Lord is doing in each generation, not just our own generation.

I remember your genuine faith, for you share the faith that first filled your grandmother Lois and your mother, Eunice. And I know that same faith continues strong in you. (2nd Timothy 1:5 NLT)

I love the fact that Timothy was one of the first second-generation Christians. He belonged to the first generation that had the Gospel message passed down to them from their parents. His mother and his grandmother were Christians, first adopters really because they were both alive in Jesus' time. I've come to realize that my kids' faith walk is unique to them, and I need to respect that and can even learn from what the Lord is teaching them along the way.

FALL

5
PAUL'S 2ND LETTER TO THE CHURCH IN CORINTH

Relying on God Through Suffering
Journal Entry   8 March 2015
Blog Entry   25 September 2019

In 2nd Corinthians 1:1-11, Paul talks about how it is sometimes difficult to serve Christ. He says that when you get to the point of so much suffering that you can't help yourself anymore, it's sort of a good thing because that's when you really begin to rely on God, which is the optimum place to live your life. If we could just live every moment in a state of knowledge of complete reliance on God, I think we would be close to living the best life we can. In reality, we live every moment relying on God, but we don't realize it. We think we are in complete control of our lives. How foolish we are!

Success or Failure is no Indicator of Godliness
Another concept that came to my mind in reading this passage was that the people in Corinth who were opposed to Paul would probably look at his problems or struggles as a reason to disqualify him as the proper leader or a

truthful leader. They might say, "Look at him. Look at the struggles he has! If he was truly blessed by God, why wouldn't God just make things easy for him and do spectacular things in his life?" It seems we tend to look up to, or revere, the people who seem to achieve greatness in this life as an example we should follow. But that's not what Jesus taught us – He didn't teach us to follow those who are wealthy and achieve great things. He taught us to love others. Just because you're not wealthy, famous, or have an easy life, doesn't mean you're not totally living the life God called you to live! The opposite is also true. If you're a wealthy superstar, it doesn't automatically mean you're doing it right either. Wealth and success in the world are totally independent of Godliness, and really have little to do with our Christian walk. But the world does look at it that way. We need to catch ourselves and not get caught up in mixing these things together. They are not interdependent!

Thank you, God, for teaching me this today, on March 8, 2015! Thank you for reminding me of it when I really needed to be reminded of this as I was typing up this note on June 12th, 2016!!Your timing is, as always, so perfect. I have been struggling for a little over a week now with an issue that is really bringing me down. I keep hearing your whispers of encouragement, but it has definitely been a battle trying to sort my brain out on this and let it go. I'm happy to see that Paul also struggled, and not everything went perfectly for him. *Not happy that he had to struggle!* However, I see that if Paul, the most amazing man of God who ever lived next to Jesus, struggled, then why wouldn't I have to struggle? Thank you, God for, your quiet assurances of hope and of being pleased with me. Please continue to bless me and push me as I press toward the goals you have for me to achieve. Help me to keep my eyes fixed on You, not on myself, my circumstances, or the circumstances of others I may be trying to help. Help me keep my eyes and my actions fixed squarely on You!

A Personal Battle with Pride, Anger, Hatred, and Confusion
Journal Entry   8 March 2015
Blog Entry   27 September 2019

Update - 27 September 2019

As I was going through my notes for today, I came across some notes I had written to God about the dark time I was going through. Even now, more than four years after the fact, I can still feel the hurt of that painful episode in my life. I had prayed for God to work on any pride issues I needed to change, and right at that time, someone hurt me, very deeply, to the core even. I feel that Satan was using this to crush me, but God used it to teach me. I thought about whether I should share this on my blog or not, as I have so far only shared my thoughts on scripture and not on my personal feelings and struggles. However, as it is my intention to save this Journal for my children and grandchildren, I thought it would be interesting and hopefully helpful for them to read. I thought it would give them a glimpse into my heart and my struggles.

Personal Diary Entry - 8 March 2015

Thank you for working on my pride issues that I have asked you to work on. It's certainly not an easy mind battle but a necessary one. I have learned that I am not God, surprise, surprise, and I am going to make mistakes, but I feel Your reassurance, telling me that it's OK at least I'm trying and that I am making progress.

As for speaking to the person who hurt me, because I am not perfect, I think it's best if I don't talk to them for a while. I feel a lot of anger and frustration toward them, and I don't want it to come out of my mouth at them so it's best if I just continue to pray for them and don't speak very much. I think I've learned through this difficult journey that I need to be quiet when I feel anger and hatred in my heart, even completely separate myself from situations that cause me to feel this way. The enemy uses these circumstances to bring me down, and there is so much good I could be doing in the world. I don't need the distractions that come from these situations to mess with my mind.

The message on the Joyce Meyer app today was entitled "Don't Take Criticism". If it comes from God, yes, I will take it. But when it comes from people, I will give it to God and ask Him to teach me what I need to learn from it. I will carry on and not worry about how that person who criticized me expects me to respond. What I will do with the mean-spirited things this particular person has said to me (over the past couple of weeks and in the past) is that I will give them to God and ask Him to teach me what he wants to teach me from this. Apart from that, I am going to let them go as the ramblings of a broken person, a person that the enemy is using to try and crush me.

As I move forward in working on pride issues in my life, please continue to help me separate what You are doing to refine me from what the enemy will use to destroy me. Thank you for this awesome time together this afternoon working this out!

Commissioned by God and Empowered by the Holy Spirit
Journal Entry   9 March 2015
Blog Entry   4 October 2019

It is God who enables us, along with you, to stand firm for Christ. He has commissioned us, and he has identified us as his own by

placing the Holy Spirit in our hearts as the first installment that guarantees everything he has promised us.
(2nd Corinthians 1:21-22 NLT)

We Each have a Job to Do in The Kingdom

Two things struck me about this passage: First, we are commissioned by God; we have a job to do. God has chosen us and placed the Holy Spirit in our hearts so that we can accomplish the work He has prepared for us to do. We've been given a responsibility in the Kingdom.

The Holy Spirit is the First Instalment of God's Promises to Us

The second thing that struck me was the idea that He has placed the Holy Spirit in our hearts as the first instalment of fulfilling all His promises. That we can know God is faithful by the presence of the Holy Spirit in our hearts and lives. When we experience the presence of the Holy Spirit, we can be assured that God has begun to work in us, and what God begins, He will bring to conclusion. We can trust that our awareness of the Holy Spirit working in us is our guarantee that there is more to come, that we are actually the children of God, and that Jesus is coming back for us.

Each One Finding Their Own Way to Faith in Christ

Journal Entry   10 March 2015
Blog Entry   7 October 2019

Paul Changes His Mind Regarding a Planned Visit to Corinth

At the end of 2 Corinthians 1, Paul tells the church at Corinth why he didn't come when he said he would. He didn't come because he was very angry with them and wanted to spare them that. He goes on the say that he didn't want to dominate them as they needed to find their own faith, which would make them steadier and give them the ability to stand stronger on their own. He adds that he will find no joy in dominating them but will be joyful to see them serving in their own strength.

It struck me that this is just the way we should treat our children when it comes to faith. I believe we can and should instruct them, but we should also make room for them to find their own way to faith so they can stand strong and serve. How joyful it makes me as a parent when I see my children strong in faith and giving time and talent to the Kingdom. However, this didn't happen by forcing them to go to church. We simply modelled a life of faith and allowed them to make their own choices when they were old enough to do so.

The reason I didn't return to Corinth was to spare you from a severe rebuke. [24] But that does not mean we want to dominate you by telling you how to put your faith into practice. We want to work together with you so you will be full of joy, for it is by your own faith that you stand firm. (2nd Corinthians 1:23-24 NLT)

Update - 7 October 2019

I originally wrote this entry on March 10, 2015, which was my eldest daughter's 24th birthday. I find it interesting that this entry happens to be about how we each find our own way to Jesus, or should I say how He finds each of us. The birth of my first child was an answer to prayer, after having suffered a miscarriage with my first pregnancy and dealing with serious infertility issues. At that time, I was new to faith, and the miracle of my daughter was the first of many miracles I would go on to experience in my journey of faith. I continue to find my way in this faith journey, but my daughter's birth was a key turning point in my faith story.

We Live by Believing not by Seeing
Journal Entry   13 March 2015
Blog Entry   9 October 2019

For we live by believing and not by seeing. (2nd Corinthians 5:7 NLT)

This seems so obvious and such a simple statement, but it is hugely powerful and has so much depth. Lately, I've been thinking a lot about how I feel, that I'm on the verge of seeing God more clearly, seeing God more clearly in the world, but it seems as if I can't, as if certain things or parts of things are hidden from me. 2nd Corinthians 5:1-10 helps me understand that in our earthly bodies, we can't know and see all the things that we will know and see in our heavenly bodies. We must continue to believe without fully seeing. However, God has given us the Holy Spirit, and this allows us to have little glimpses of heaven here and there in our day-to-day life.

The Presence of the Holy Spirit Moving in our Lives is our Guarantee of God's Truth

Just as Paul told us in 2nd Corinthians 1:21-22, he tells us again in 2nd Corinthians 5:5 that God has given us the Holy Spirit as a guarantee toward what is to come.

Paul says God has given us the "deposit" of the Holy Spirit, or has deposited the Holy Spirit in us, and this is the down-payment God makes with us that we will see much greater things. We need to be patient and keep on believing, keep journeying, until that day comes when we will see everything clearly.

Made Right with God Through Christ
Journal Entry   13 March 2015
Blog Entry   11 October 2019

In this part of the letter, Paul admonishes the Corinthians to reach out to others and tell them about God and the reconciliation He offers. To tell others about the free gift God gave us in Jesus so that we could be reconciled to Him. He advises that we shouldn't take this responsibility lightly.

As God's partners, we beg you not to accept this marvellous gift of God's kindness and then ignore it.
(2nd Corinthians 6:1 NLT)

Living the Heavenly Life While Still Being Here on Earth

There is so much more to the Christian life than receiving salvation. Of course, salvation in itself is too amazing for words, and too great for the human brain to understand. Though hard to believe, there is even more God has offered us through Christ's sacrifice. He has opened up a new life for us while we are still here in these earthly bodies. This gift is not only for entry to Heaven; it's for entry to Heavenly life here on earth from the moment we receive Jesus.

However, in order to live this heavenly life, you need to actually participate with God. You can't simply receive eternal life and then ignore it. I guess you actually can, but you would miss out on so, so much. Receiving it and then ignoring this free gift, ignoring God in your life here on earth, will seal your salvation but will deny you all the wonder God has for you in the here and now.

When I pay attention to it, I can almost see and feel Christ's light shining out from me, but I need to invest in the relationship and take time with God to keep this light shining. When I ignore God, even for a day or two, the light starts to grow dim, and the thorns begin to grow over my heart.

Then Jesus said to his disciples, "If any of you wants to be my follower, you must give up your own way, take up your cross, and follow me. ²⁵ If you try to hang on to your life, you will lose it. But if you give up your life for my sake, you will save it.
(Matthew 16:24-25 NLT)

I believe this is the essence of this verse. If you lose your life for Christ, by allowing His light to shine out through you and staying in a close relationship with Him, you actually find your real life here on earth. The life you were meant to live, the abundant life! So, it's better to ignore your old life and continue on in this new life with Christ in control and the Holy Spirit leading your way!

Serving Through Hardship
Journal Entry   23 March 2015
Blog Entry   14 October 2019

Paul writes about the hardships he has experienced, not to make the Corinthians feel sorry for him but to show by example how we can give up all worldly things but still have everything we need. Paul demonstrates that when we put God first, we always have everything we need.

We have been beaten, but we have not been killed. ¹⁰ Our hearts ache, but we always have joy.
(2nd Corinthians 6:9-10 NLT)

Update - 14 October 2019 - Thanksgiving

I have so, so much to be thankful for, and this holiday reminds me of just how blessed I am. However, there have been various times in my life when things were difficult. Something I learned along the way was that the one constant in my journey has always been a loving God walking with me through every experience. When I finally began to learn to put God first in my life, I was able to handle difficult situations with hope. I learned that hardship is not the time to give up on God. God doesn't want us to suffer. Rather, God wants us to lean closer in to Him in the tough times. No matter what comes, we can always choose to close our eyes and feel the arms of our Lord wrapping around us in love and listen for the whisper of the Holy Spirit directing our steps. No one can ever take that away from us, and that is truly something to be thankful for!

Generous Giving and God's Economy
Journal Entry   25 March 2015
Blog Entry   16 October 2019

Still super cold outside. We've had a near interminable winter this year! This morning's reading for me was 2 Corinthians 8. In this passage, Paul talks to the church in Corinth about giving. A timely passage for me as we just got our income tax refund, and I'm about to catch up on my tithe, which I am behind on for this year! Paul says to honour your commitment, to give enthusiastically and not out of a motive to get something in return. Also, to give until it hurts, but not at the expense of providing for your family.

You Can't Out-give God
I believe that I give my tithe out of duty, but also knowing that by doing this, God will provide for all our needs. I have seen Him rescue us time and time again when we had nothing left in our bank account. I've seen Him supernaturally provide where we saw no provision on the horizon. A Christian friend once told me, years ago, about God's economy. I live, depend, and have peace based on this principle. The principle is that you can never out-give God. I'm certain this sounds like foolishness to those who don't know God and haven't been able to fully place their trust in God. Unfortunately, if you can never get to the

point where you can fully trust God with your finances, you'll never see the amazing financial miracles we see.

The Living Room Miracle

I remember one time when we had no extra money, and our living room was a wreck. I mean a real wreck. I would never have anyone over because our carpets were soaked with stains, and our furniture was all falling apart. Anyway, I prayed that morning for help for our decrepit living room.

My husband got home from work before I did that day, and he called me at work and asked if I had been praying for money. I said no, but that I had prayed for help with the living room. He said that he had received a completely unexpected cheque from his previous employer for $6,000. I knew God had sent us this money for the room. We used it all for that. We put in hardwood floors, painted, and bought furniture. It's funny because we ended up having our teenagers' youth group friends over a few times after that, and that's where they hung out. I remember thinking God had provided us a nice place where they could meet and honour Him and praise His name. It was such an incredible experience to see and hear them praying, laughing, and singing worship songs in that room He had provided!

Cheerful Giving
Journal Entry   26 March 2015
Blog Entry   18 October 2019

In 2nd Corinthians 9, Paul is talking to the Corinthians about their initial excitement and enthusiasm to give to others. He reminds them that they have inspired others by their zeal to give but also reminds them not to embarrass themselves, or Paul, by not following up on their commitments. The Lord loves a cheerful giver passage is in here. The idea is that God wants us to give enthusiastically, not grudgingly or out of fear, or just out of a sense of arduous duty. I've heard it said that the words here could be interpreted to mean that God wants us to give hilariously!

You must each decide in your heart how much to give. And don't give reluctantly or in response to pressure. "For God loves a person who gives cheerfully."⁸ And God will generously provide all you need. Then you will always have everything you need and plenty left over to share with others. (2nd Corinthians 9:7-8 NLT)

It's a heart matter; yes, it's our responsibility and duty to give, but we shouldn't resent giving. If we do resent it, then our heart is not yet in the right place, and we should pray that God will work in us and change our attitude toward giving to others.

This is the week I catch up on my yearly tithing, so this is timely information for me! Also, this morning I was reminded by my daughter's experience in her class yesterday, that discipline is required and often the precursor to great joy!

My eldest daughter is an elementary school teacher. Yesterday, she had to bring her students back to the classroom from the gym for a time-out. Afterward, they were able to go back to the gym and enjoy a better gym period than usual. As she told me this story, I sensed the Holy Spirit reminding me that I need to be disciplined in my eating, exercising, and even spending and giving habits so that I would enjoy an amazing retirement! We reap the seeds we sow!

Remember this—a farmer who plants only a few seeds will get a small crop. But the one who plants generously will get a generous crop. (2nd Corinthians 9:6 NLT)

World's Authority vs God's Authority
Journal Entry   27 March 2015
Blog Entry 21   October 2019

In the last few chapters of Paul's second letter to the Corinthians, Paul is defending his authority to preach to them. Paul is defending himself against criticism that apparently some are making of him that he writes boldly but can't speak as well publicly.

The city of Corinth was in Greece, and the Greek culture was very proud of their intellect and human abilities as orators. Many of them may have been judging Paul with those human standards. Paul wasn't among their elite, so I believe what his critics were saying was not to listen to him because he really wasn't that worthy of their attention.

Paul tries to explain that there are two different standards one can be judged by, worldly standards and God's standards. According to God's standards, Paul had immense authority; he had actually talked to Jesus and was relaying Jesus' message to the world. Can't get much more important than that! However, by the world's standards, Paul didn't have much authority. This isn't what matters when we are delivering God's word. We should remember not to give too much weight to what the world thinks of us and depend on what God thinks of us.

Satan Disguised as an Angel of Light
Journal Entry   31 March 2015
Blog Entry   23 October 2019

But I am not surprised! Even Satan disguises himself as an angel of light. (2nd Corinthians 11:14 NLT)

In this part of 2nd Corinthians, Chapters 10 and 11, Paul defends his authority as there are many false prophets trying to deceive the Corinthians. Paul is giving them his credentials and telling them that those who teach a different gospel aren't to be followed.

A Personal Experience with Deception
I get the symbolism here that these false preachers are disguising themselves as truthful but are only after money or some other gain for themselves. However, the thing that stuck out for me personally was the idea of Satan disguising himself as an angel of light. I thought back to the memory of an experience I had in 2004. I was on morphine after an emergency C-section I had undergone during the birth of my fourth child.

The "Dream"
In the dream, I was flying or floating in a dark, drippy cave that went up and down forever. There was no bottom and no top. The cave was littered with repulsive gargoyles, and I knew that I had to keep looking for Jesus. I felt my mission in there was to look for Jesus. I wasn't scared because I felt sure I would find Him, and He would find me.

Then, I saw this beautiful angel of light in the middle of all of this darkness, but I knew immediately that this wasn't Jesus, that it was Satan disguising himself as Jesus. He was calling me to come to him, but I refused and said, "No, you're not Jesus. Jesus will come to find me, so I'll wait for him." I remember feeling surprised that I wasn't afraid. I was very confident and secure in knowing Jesus would come for me.

During the dream, I also remember thinking about the scripture in John 10:3-5: "I am the shepherd, and the sheep know my voice." I didn't know exactly where it was in the Bible during this experience, but I knew that was a verse somewhere in the Bible. I was confident that this being that looked exactly like an angel of light, and looked like the only beautiful, right, and good thing in all this vast darkness, was indeed not the Shepherd. Somehow, even though my eyes and my great desire to get out of this darkness were looking right at this beautiful light calling me, I could tell right away in my spirit that it was fake.

When I finally woke up, I remembered this "dream" I had had. It's still pretty clear to this day, and it really strengthened my faith. I felt very sure after that dream that I will know Jesus when He calls me, that I don't have to worry about being deceived and following the wrong voice.

I am the good shepherd; I know my own sheep, and they know me (John 10:14 NLT)

Earthly Success is no Indicator of Godliness
Journal Entry   1 April 2015
Blog Entry   25 October 2019

In wrapping up his second letter to the Corinthians, in chapters 10 through 12, Paul tells them about his authority as an apostle. He recounts all he has done and been through while expending himself completely to bring the Gospel to the various cultures. His motive for doing this is to help them see clearly that the false apostles, who are trying to lead them astray and lead them away from Paul, are lying to them. Paul is hoping they will see that the false apostles who tell them Paul is not to be trusted or followed are deceitful.

The thing that struck me this morning while reading this was that Paul, who gave his entire life and being to teach the Gospel and reach the nations, still suffered immensely. However, in spite of this suffering, he continued to trust God and follow the leading of the Holy Spirit. I believe that sometimes people think that if their lives aren't completely blessed or going perfectly, it means they are doing something wrong, or aren't devoted enough to Christ. But look at Paul! So many things went wrong but God was still loving him, honouring him, and blessing him, and was ever present in his life. Just because life is a struggle doesn't mean we aren't in the right place with God. It could mean this, but it doesn't necessarily mean this. Success or failure in our culture isn't an accurate indicator of Godliness.

Staying Perfectly on the Right Path

I remembered thinking about this concept before, that how much money we have, or how much we suffer, may have nothing to do with whether we are in the right place with God. I looked back and found that my blog post for Chapter 1 of 2nd Corinthians also talked about this idea. Being somewhat of a perfectionist, this concept is very comforting for me. My life doesn't have to be perfect to be perfectly following Jesus. My job is to stay in the Word, serve in the community, love my neighbour, and trust the Holy Spirit to guide me through each day. No matter what each day looks like on the outside, as long as I'm following that recipe, I'll stay on the right path perfectly.

6
PAUL'S LETTER TO THE CHURCH IN GALATIA

Works Versus Faith
Journal Entry   8 April 2015
Blog Entry   30 October 2019

This is my first entry for the book of Galatians. I love the candidness of this book. It says what it needs to, with no sugar coating or beating around the bush. When I was taking a course at University in Christian writing, the professor told us that Galatians is the only letter Paul wrote that does not include Paul's customary opening of thanksgiving for the church to whom he is writing. We were taught that Paul left this out deliberately as he was not happy with the church in Galatia. He was alarmed over their theological situation and wanted to get straight to the point of his letter. The point being that they were in danger of accepting a different gospel that was being preached among them that would lead to the ruin of their souls. The study notes in my Life Application Bible refer to it this way:

"Paul is defending the gospel of justification by faith alone, true gospel vs a false gospel; faith vs works; law vs. grace; liberty vs legalism; Sonship vs slavery; and the fruit of the Spirit vs the desires of the flesh."

In Galatians 3:2, Paul asks this question, *"Did you receive the Holy Spirit by obeying the law? Of course not, you received the Holy Spirit because you believed the message you heard about Christ."*

God Shows up Through Faith Alone
This passage struck me because, through my faith journey, I have had many, many experiences of God's presence in my life. In these moments, I experience what I call Holy

Spirit shivers. It's hard to explain, but it's just this overwhelming feeling like no other that God is present and is actively working things out. This feeling is usually accompanied by physical tingling or shivers.

When one of my sons was fourteen, we received some extremely disappointing news regarding his future direction. That week, during worship on Sunday, I had this experience of God saying to me, "Don't worry, I've got him; he's mine."

Another time, when I found out I was pregnant when I was 42, I was astounded. I had very difficult pregnancies and really wasn't expecting this. However, I heard God telling me that this child was His plan. I ended up needing an emergency C-section. The thought crossed my mind that I might not make it through, but I really was completely calm. I felt confident that whatever happened, it was God's plan, and His plan was way better than mine.

Those are just two examples, but there have been so many instances of experiencing this strong, tangible sense of the Holy Spirit working in my life, of hearing His still small voice reassuring me.

Now, did I have those experiences because I kept the law? Because I measured up to some kind of standard God has set? No, I had those experiences because I choose to believe and put my hopes and faith in Christ. That is the key! I don't have to *do* anything to receive the promise of the Holy Spirit, to hear the Holy Spirit speak into my life. I just have to *believe* in the one who sent Him and the one who died so that I could hear Him.

Dying to Self and Living a New Life
Journal Entry   9 April 2015
Blog Entry   1 November 2019

My old self has been crucified with Christ, it is no longer I who live but Christ lives in me.
(Galatians: 2:20 NLT)

Lately, I'm having a new revelation of this. I think it started one day in church a few months ago. I felt the Holy Spirit prompt me to just keep repeating over and over in worship, *It's not about me; it's about You, Jesus.*

It's Not About Me; It's About You, Jesus.

I think I'm finally starting to understand what it means to die to self. It's really letting go of who you are by letting go of your past, your plans, your everything, and trusting Jesus to take over and lead you—giving it all to Him because He died to save you. Your life before Jesus, that old life, that dull life, that plastic life, is no good to you anyway, it only leads to death. So you need to consciously, intentionally, give God every part of your life and watch what He does with it! Your life will be so much more amazing than what you could ever have done with it. As I'm writing this, I'm suddenly thinking of a brother who gave up on church and admittedly has a pretty good life. So I'm thinking he has a good life and he doesn't believe. However, then I think that his life would even be better, even greater than it is if he did choose to believe.

Thank you, God, Jesus, Holy Spirit, for helping me go deeper and deeper in understanding Your word and the life you died to give me. Thank you for opening the eyes of my heart and mind to see and experience new things, new mindsets, things that I couldn't see before and that no one is able to see without Your help. Please continue to show me more and more, bring me deeper and deeper, to be more fully alive for you every day!

Differences Between Having Faith and Obeying

the Law
Journal Entry 10 April 2015
Blog Entry 5 November 2019

In Galatians 3:15-21, Paul explains the differences between the "Law" and "Faith". He says that God gave Abraham promises because of his faith, not because of his obedience to the law. In the same way, God delivers on the promises He made to us in His word because of our faith in Jesus, not because of anything we do.

God gave us His laws to show us how best to live, but not as a requirement to receive the fulfilment of His promises. We are the recipients of His promises simply by believing in God, in His plan for salvation. No goodness of our own doing or work is required. We are heirs. We are his family, Christ's descendants, simply by trusting God's promises. He knows each one of us better than anyone, and He knew He couldn't save us any other way. He knew that we would sin at some point in our lives. He planned out our salvation this way, through Christ, because this is the only way we can't fail. All we need to do is to believe!

While pondering on this idea, I thought about Exodus and the Ten Commandments, and the *Prince of Egypt* movies, specifically, the part where the Israelites are busy making idols at the base of the mountain and Moses comes down the mountain with the Ten Commandments. I had always seen it as God being mad at them because Moses was mad at them. But today, I see that God wasn't angry with them. He was simply giving them instructions on how to live, because clearly, they needed to know! He gave them the Ten Commandments out of love to help them live better lives, not as a prerequisite to being blessed or knowing Him, or getting closer to Him. We get blessed and receive God's promises not by meeting any standard, but by believing alone, by genuine faith, by choosing to honour

God in our lives.

Update - 5 November 2019

This is such a hard concept for me to accept, that I am part of God's family based *only* on the fact that *I choose to believe in Jesus* and his sacrifice for me. However, an incident that happened to me in March 2016 plays over in my head when doubts start creeping into my mind.

I'm God's Daughter, Not His servant!
Journal Entry from 7 March 2016
"This morning, I woke up with a new perspective on who I am in Christ. I'm God's daughter! I'm not His servant. I used to wake up in the morning and ask God to help me be His faithful servant that day. But when I prayed that prayer this morning, I clearly heard God tell me that I'm not His servant in the world; I'm His daughter! That gave me a sense of elevation and power, like I need to grab hold of some things that have been keeping me down and give them a shake!"

The Law Versus The Promise
Journal Entry   12 April 2015
Blog Entry   6 November 2019

Galatians 4
All through Galatians, there's a tension between the "law" and "grace". It is a difficult concept to wrap your head around. Paul tells us we are saved by grace and therefore completely free. We are no longer slaves to the law. The law was given to show us the standard we would have to achieve to be completely right with God and also to show us that no human could ever do this! This law showed us that every single one of us falls short and is in need of a Saviour. The law wasn't meant as a standard we could meet, but as a guideline. When we fall short, we receive the

mercy of God, through Christ, for our failings.

Update 6 November 2019

I read Galatians 4 over and over in various versions this morning. The part that stuck out for me today was the allegory Paul offers regarding Hagar's child and Sarah's child.

The Scriptures say that Abraham had two sons, one from his slave wife and one from his freeborn wife. The son of the slave wife was born in a human attempt to bring about the fulfilment of God's promise. But the son of the freeborn wife was born as God's own fulfilment of his promise. (Galatians 4:22-23 NLT)

"And we, [believing] brothers and sisters, like Isaac, are children [not merely of physical descent, like Ishmael, but are children born] of promise [born miraculously]." (Galatians 4:28 AMP)

Father God, help me to completely and fully receive Your gift of my miraculous rebirth into Your promise. Let this understanding of who I am in Christ go down deep into my soul and spirit so that I no longer strive to please You but live freely to glorify You!

Live Your Life Guided by the Holy Spirit's Lead (Die to Self)
Journal Entry   13 April 2015
Blog Entry   8 November 2019

So, I say let the Holy Spirit guide your lives, then you won't be doing what your sinful nature craves. (Galatians 5:16 NLT)

This is a great scripture for me always, but right now, particularly. I am really hearing God, through His Holy Spirit, telling me to exercise, eat properly, and the result will be losing weight, but the result will also be an emotionally, physically, mentally, and spiritually bountiful life! I can already see and experience some of the wonderful peace and feeling of fulfilment God has for me when I choose to obey the guiding of the Holy Spirit. It is hard to submit and give up what I want and instead follow His lead and His still small voice directing me, but it is more than worth it. I am certain that if I don't do it, refuse to follow His lead, I will miss out on so much! I will completely forfeit the beauty He is standing ready to pour out on my life over the ashes of my past.

Crucified with Christ? What Does that Mean?
Recently, the Lord has been teaching me what crucified with Christ means. I never quite understood that before. I couldn't understand how I could die with Christ, as He died on the cross, while here I am still very much alive many thousands of years later.

I think I'm starting to understand this whole idea of dying to self. To die to self is to really live the life God intended for you and had planned for you! It's about every little decision you make all day long, every day. You give those thoughts and decisions and choices over to Christ, and you listen to what the Holy Spirit is telling you. You then consciously make the choice you know the Holy Spirit tells you to make. It's not easy, as you want to do what you want to do, and it ends up a battle of will. Also, it's a bit more stressful at first, at least for me, because I don't want to think that much or be disciplined. I just want the freedom to do what I want to do in the moment.

Experiencing Real Peace
When I do make the choices, the Holy Spirit is calling me to make, I have this supernatural sense of calm, freedom, and peace. It's a feeling that is very hard to articulate. The only thing I can compare it to is the sense of wonder, freedom, and happiness I remember feeling as a five-year-

old girl walking home from school. It's a carefree feeling. An inner sense that everything is beautiful and wonderful in the world, and you're just waiting for the next great and wonderful thing to happen. I've been missing that feeling for 50 years now! Maybe as children, we can hear the Holy Spirit more clearly because the strife of the world hasn't started blocking Him out yet. I feel that when I stay in tune with the Holy Spirit, I start to get that sense of wonder and freedom back.

What am I personally Being Called to Do Right Now?

Things Holy Spirit has been calling me to do just in recent months; pay off debt, save 10% (we never saved before, so this is new and will hopefully help us not to run out of money before the next paycheque), tithe 10%, eat properly, exercise regularly, don't get into gossipy discussions at work or at home, slow down, reduce stress and enjoy time with the kids more, cut back work hours.

I'm trusting God will help us manoeuvre the reduced income and still help us pay off the enormous debt we have right now. This debt was at $107,000 at its peak! Those are the big things, but I also try to tune into the daily guidance of the Holy Spirit. For instance, today I was doing some cleaning, and I heard the Holy Spirit ask me to take some time out to sit on the porch, read the word and write. So, I stopped housework, with at least 30 minutes left before the kids were to come home from school, to soak in God's presence and write.

Christ has set us free to enjoy our freedom. So remain strong in the faith. Don't let the chains of slavery hold you again. (Galatian 5:1 NIRV)

Don't go back to bondage. When you fall, start again. Eventually, you will get better at it and be more consistent. Then you will begin to see God's blessings pour out in abundance. Put God first in everything, and all things will then be given unto you! It's a process. Focus on how far you've come, not how far you have yet to go.

Update - 8 November 2019

As I read over today's entry, I felt that some people might misunderstand, thinking that I am now in slavery to the Holy Spirit! How can I say I'm free if I am taking the time to capture every thought and give it over to the Holy Spirit for direction? However, that is the deception from the enemy that we need to fight. Our spiritual enemy tricks us into thinking we are free if we can just do whatever we feel like doing. However, when we do that, we are actually in bondage to our enemy Satan. If the Holy Spirit is not directing our thoughts, the enemy is. We will always belong to one spiritual ruler or another. We have the power to choose life or death. Please choose life!

Further evidence of God's goodness when we follow the right voice: 4.5 years after writing today's original entry, the $107,000 debt is completely gone, and I've lost 40 lbs! Our God is not just very good; He is more than amazing!

Don't Get Tired of Doing Good
Journal Entry   4 March 2019
Blog Entry   11 November 2019

So let's not get tired of doing what is good. At just the right time we will reap a harvest of blessing if we don't give up.
(Galatians 6:9 NLT)

This scripture just keeps coming up over and over in my life. An elderly lady who attended the church in my hometown (the same church we had attended more than 25 years ago) even gave me a little fridge magnet she had made herself with part of this verse written in her own handwriting. She died many years ago, but I still have this little homemade magnet bearing her scrawly writing. It's not lost on me that the Lord is trying to get this message through to me!

A few weeks ago, actually, on February 22, 2019, while I was exercising, a new thing the Lord has been doing in my life since the Fall of 2018, He asked me to write a song about my understanding of this verse. So, I thought I'd come to my notes, from my two years of going through the Bible, and see what I had written about Gal 6:9. Here I am looking for it, and there is nothing! Lord, you are so much fun to follow. I had been putting off looking this up, and then when I finally get here, I find nothing. I had written nothing on my understanding of this verse, even though it's one of the few verses I have memorized.

I still think you want me to write a song on this verse as I very clearly heard your Spirit prompting me to do this. I'll just have to wait until You give me the understanding and the lyrics you want me to write for this song because I don't have a clue what to write.

Update 11 November 2019 - Sowing and Reaping

No song written yet, but as I came to Galatians 6:9 today in my blog, it is speaking to me about sowing and reaping. I have found it's often difficult to keep trusting and believing when you can't see the results of your efforts. I think this verse is meant to motivate and encourage us to keep going, keep believing, keep in the word, close to God, obeying the lead of the Holy Spirit, and above all else, don't give up. The Biblical principle of sowing and reaping can be trusted. Even if you don't see results yet, eventually, you will. The truth is the truth; what you sow, you will reap. So, keep sowing good seeds and look forward to the amazing harvest to come!

7
PAUL'S LETTER TO THE CHURCH IN EPHESUS

The Holy Spirit - God's Down Payment and Guarantee
Journal Entry   15 April 2015
Blog Entry   13 November 2019

Starting the book of Ephesians today – Paul's letter to the church in Ephesus. I did a little research and found that contrary to some of the other letters Paul wrote to various churches, this letter was not written to address any particular problem in the church. Paul was very close to the Ephesians, having spent three years there ministering to them. The purpose of the letter was to strengthen the believers and explain the nature and purpose of the Church, the body of Christ, in general. One interesting fact I found is that the city of Ephesus had a general fascination with magic and the occult, hence Paul's emphasis on the supreme power of God over all things. Paul reminds his readers of the constant battle being waged over the forces of darkness and encourages the church to use every spiritual weapon at their disposal to fight.

The Holy Spirit
When you believed, you were marked in him with a seal, the promised Holy Spirit, [14] who is a deposit guaranteeing our inheritance until the redemption of those who are God's possession (Ephesians 1:14 NIV)

Paul tells the Ephesians that the Holy Spirit is God's guarantee that He will give the inheritance He has promised, and that He has purchased us to be His own people! How comforting is that! I can't deny that I have felt the Holy Spirit working and directing my steps many times in my life. The mere fact that I have experienced the presence of the Holy Spirit assures me that God's promises are true. The Holy Spirit is the down payment on the rest that's yet to come.

Update - 13 November 2019

As I was writing this entry up today, I was sure I had written about the Holy Spirit being God's guarantee before, so I looked back and found it in my entry for October 9, 2019. Paul also told the church in Corinth this same truth in 2nd Corinthians 1:21-22, and again in 2nd Corinthians 5:5.

Paul says God has given us the "deposit" of the Holy Spirit, or has deposited the Holy Spirit in us, and this is the down-payment God makes with us that we will see much greater things. We need to be patient and keep on believing, keep journeying, until that day comes when we will see everything clearly.

Reverence for God
Journal Entry   20 April 2015
Blog Entry   15 November 2019

Little departure from Ephesians this morning.

I woke up this morning with a revelation that we could be living out God's purpose for our lives without doing anything outstanding or famous. As long as we are obedient to Him and putting Him first in our lives every day, we will accomplish His will for our lives, even if it doesn't look like it to us.

I think I've always had this preoccupation with *fame*. But in my heart today, I heard God whisper that it's not about being famous or popular; it's about Him, not about me, and it's about putting Him first every day. Even if we never become rich or famous or popular, we will have lived the life we were intended to live as long as we simply put Him first every day.

My youngest daughter wanted to read the book of Malachi at bedtime last night, and so far, (chapters 1 and 2), the book is about reverence for God. I started thinking about what that means. What does having reverence for God really mean? It seems to me that putting Him first in our lives and having reverence for Him are connected but still a bit different.

Reverence
I realized that I've been struggling with the reverence part of it lately. I want my mind to give God the worship and reverence He so deserves, but for some reason, my mind, imagination, and brain can't seem to go there. I was sitting here pondering this in God's presence this morning, and it occurred to me that I have never really had reverence for anyone. All the authority figures in my life either disappointed or hurt me. It suddenly occurred to me that perhaps this is a part of the reason I have trouble properly "revering" God. I've never had an example of anyone or anything worth revering and have no practical experience with reverence. Then again, no one in this world could ever even come close to deserving the kind of reverence we should have for God. Also, there is just the plain old mystery of God and who He is that makes it difficult to adequately grasp all He is. Our human brain being finite can't get it, so it's difficult to appropriately honour God when we can't see or understand Him.

[5] *"The purpose of my covenant with the Levites was to bring life and peace, and that is what I gave them. This required reverence from them, and they greatly revered me and stood in awe of my*

name. *⁶ They passed on to the people the truth of the instructions they received from me. They did not lie or cheat; they walked with me, living good and righteous lives, and they turned many from lives of sin. (Malachi 2:5-6 NLT)*

God's Spirit Alive in Us, His Church
Journal Entry   20 April 2015
Blog Entry   18 November 2019

In church this week, we learned that "The Church" is a movement (of people), not a building. We have mistakenly made it into a building. Ephesians 2:21-22 also confirms this, that Christ's temple, His church, are people, not buildings, where God's Spirit lives in hearts.

¹⁹ So now you Gentiles are no longer strangers and foreigners. You are citizens along with all of God's holy people. You are members of God's family. ²⁰ Together, we are his house, built on the foundation of the apostles and the prophets. And the cornerstone is Christ Jesus himself. ²¹ We are carefully joined together in him, becoming a holy temple for the Lord. ²² Through him you Gentiles are also being made part of this dwelling where God lives by his Spirit.
(Ephesians 2:19-22 NLT)

Update - 18 November 2019

In Ephesians 2:1-17, Paul explains to the Gentiles (anyone not born into a Jewish family) that God has saved us by sending Christ to die for our sins, which opened the door for the Holy Spirit to live in our hearts. When we choose to put our faith in Christ, believe in Him, and the sacrifice He made for us, this opens the door for the Holy Spirit to start speaking to our thoughts and directing our decisions. Prior to this act of saving grace, which God has done for us, we were all directed by our enemy, the devil.

² You used to live in sin, just like the rest of the world, obeying the devil—the commander of the powers in the unseen world. He is the spirit at work in the hearts of those who refuse to obey God. ³ All of us used to live that way, following the passionate desires and inclinations of our sinful nature. By our very nature we were subject to God's anger, just like everyone else. (Ephesians 2:2-3 NLT)

So, there is a clear choice for us. We can choose to keep being directed by the devil, or we can choose to be directed by God. This was a theme Paul wrote about back in Galatians as well. The thing that strikes me today is that there is no middle ground. In the spiritual world, we either belong to the devil or to God. If we choose not to accept Christ's sacrifice, which releases the Holy Spirit's guidance over our lives, we aren't free to be ourselves, or in the middle, we belong to the devil. There are only two options, not three.

"So I say let the Holy Spirit guide your lives, then you won't be doing what your sinful nature craves." (Galatians 5:16 NLT)

Thank you, God, that out of your beautiful love and heart for us, you made a way for us to be free from the devil's grasp. Help us to hear Your voice above the noise of the enemy's schemes and plots.

The Trap - Our Sinful Nature
Journal Entry   21 April 2015
Blog Entry   20 November 2019

Throw off your old sinful nature and your former way of life, which is corrupted by lust and deception. Instead let the Spirit renew your thoughts and attitudes. (Ephesians 4:22-23 NLT)

I love this scripture. It helps me realize that I need to shake off my former attitudes about so many things! About eating and exercising, spending and managing money, foul language, foul jokes, all those uncontrolled behaviours that are really a deceptive way of living, a corrupted way of living. It is hard because that's what my nature wants me to do; it is what I "know" best and what I feel most comfortable doing. But it is not what God intended for me and is truly not the most effective and glorious way to live.

It seems more natural and easier to live this way, but in reality, it will make our lives more difficult and painful. If I don't eat right and exercise, I don't feel good and will be in much pain and disease as I age. If I don't manage money well, I will be burdened with the stress of worrying about how I will survive.

Escaping our Sinful Nature

Our sinful nature is such a trap! We must escape in order to live our best lives. The only way to get free is to receive the rescue Christ provided for us on the cross. His sacrifice opened the door for us to put on our new nature and ask the Holy Spirit to renew our minds. The Holy Spirit only came after Christ's death. If Jesus had not sacrificed Himself to release the Holy Spirit, we would have no ability to free ourselves from our sinful nature. Let's not waste this amazing opportunity God has given us by sacrificing His son!

Update - 20 November 2019

Live no longer as the Gentiles do, for they are hopelessly confused. [18] Their minds are full of darkness; they wander far from the life God gives because they have closed their minds and hardened their hearts against him. (Ephesians 4:17-18 NLT)

As I was reading over Ephesians 4 today in preparation for writing my blog post, these verses jumped out for me. I've found it to be so true that when I lose sight of the Holy Spirit and start falling into my sinful nature patterns, I feel confused and lost. Even though acting according to my sinful nature is more familiar to me and easy to slip into, mentally, it does feel darker and more confusing when compared to my mental state when I'm operating within God's will for my life. There is a heaviness that is lifted; it's as if there's a dark heavy blanket covering me but when I allow the Holy Spirit to lead, the darkness and heaviness are removed from me.

Jesus' Death on the Cross Sets Everyone Free!
Journal Entry   4 March 2017
Blog Entry   22 November 2019

Jesus set you free from the grip of sin and darkness by the sacrificial death He died on the cross.

As I was typing out my notes on Ephesians 4, the Holy Spirit revealed to me that whether you believe in Jesus or not, this reality is still true for you. Just because you don't believe in Him doesn't mean that this opportunity of freedom isn't available and already present in your life.

Christ Set You Free - This is a Fact, a Truth, Whether You Choose to Believe it or Not

We are all walking in this freedom that Christ gave us. However, most of us don't even realize or acknowledge that the only reason we can do this is because of what He did for us on the cross. Just because you don't acknowledge Him doesn't mean that it didn't happen, nor does it mean that you aren't set free by it. It's just sad because you think you did it on your own. You think you've accomplished all you have done by yourself, and fail to thank the one who made it possible for you to live the life you have.

Thank you, Jesus, for all you have done for all of us, and for forgiving us when we forget to acknowledge you and your enormous sacrifice for us!

Three weeks after I wrote the little note above, I finally got back to typing out my 2015 notes and realized that the Holy Spirit had sent me this insight just in time for a discussion that came up with my oldest son.

I was philosophizing with my oldest son (we always get into these super deep discussions). He was talking about how God lives in our hearts, but we often miss Him because we have so much stuff that clutters up our lives and distracts us. He believed that if we can find God inside us, that place of peace where He lives in us and is trying to shine out of us, that's what is really key to having a great life.

Jesus Opened the Spiritual Door for Us
I told him I agreed with this, that God is inside us, and the only way we are able to get rid of that junk that clouds our spiritual eyes from seeing Him is through accepting what Jesus did on the cross for us. If Jesus hadn't opened that spiritual door for us, we would never have even a hope of throwing off the deadly and sinful junk. We would be so weighted down and blinded by darkness that we wouldn't be able to find God in ourselves. However, because of what Jesus did, He made it possible for us to truly live, to really find God living in us, to realize just how much He really loves us and wants us to live amazing lives.

Cracks of Light
Once we start to see that light, there's no going back. Little by little, it starts to shine out through us. But as I said above, I think this happens to people in various religions. They can start to see this light and start doing wonderful works in the world, but the only reason they are able to do this is because of the door Christ opened. They just don't realize that they wouldn't have been able to do it without Christ's sacrifice. They think they are able to do it on their

own or by obeying various false teachings. However, in truth, they really wouldn't be able to do the good things they are doing and have the peace and love they have if Jesus hadn't gone to the cross and defeated darkness on their behalf.

Don't be Drunk With Wine. It will Ruin Your Life!
Journal Entry   23 April 2015
Blog Entry   25 November 2019

Don't be drunk with wine for that will ruin your life. Instead, be filled with the Holy Spirit.
(Ephesians 5:18 NLT)

Ephesians 5:18 really popped out for me, as alcohol has played such a significant and terrible role in my childhood, having caused immense problems for several of my family members. I have always seen alcohol as an enemy that ruined most of my childhood.

In the Life Application Bible, the notes state that Paul is again contrasting getting drunk with wine as the old way, the sinful self, and comparing that to living in the Spirit, metaphorically saying we can have that feeling of euphoria, giddiness, and happiness that makes us want to sing by being full of the Holy Spirit rather than being physically drunk on wine. As light bearers, we have to refrain from all those old, destructive habits.

For me, the meaning of this is twofold: in the physical world, being an alcoholic ruins your life. I have seen that happen first-hand in my own family. Secondly, this is another attempt by Paul to help us contrast our old nature with our new self in Christ. I love Ephesians!

Instructions for Husbands and Wives
Journal Entry   27 April 2015
Blog Entry   27 November 2019

I spent a few days mulling over Ephesians 5:25-33, which talks about a Spirit-guided relationship between husbands and wives. This teaching is also given in 1 Peter 3:1-7 and in Colossians 3:18-19.

This principle is that the husband is the head of his wife, and the wife is to submit to her husband. This is perhaps a difficult concept in our society where feminism runs rampant! However, as mentioned earlier, submission doesn't mean inferiority; it means order.

God's Order for the Family Unit

God's order for the family unit is for the husband to be the head and the wife to submit to his authority. We see an example of this kind of order in Christ's submission to the father. Christ is not less than God but submitted to His authority in order to bring about the salvation of the world. Amazing things can be done when God's order is followed! Also, husbands are to love their wives as Christ loved the church. This is a self-sacrificing love, a willingness even to die for their wives. Back to submission; another item I found in researching this passage was that wives are to submit to their husbands but not to other men. The Bible doesn't put "men" in charge of all women but is speaking here to the husband-wife and family relationship.

Marriage - Not Just One in Flesh, but One in Spirit

Finally, Paul teaches us here that marriage is sacred and it results in two people becoming one flesh, not in the physical sense, which is the way I always thought of it but in the spiritual sense. In the spiritual sense, once married, we are one. I always still thought of us as two but want to begin to remember this concept of us being one in spirit!

In the same way, you husbands must give honour to your wives. Treat your wife with understanding as you live together. She may be weaker than you are, but she is your equal partner in God's gift of new life. (1 Peter 3:7 NLT)

In the same way, you wives must accept the authority of your husbands. Then, even if some refuse to obey the Good News, your godly lives will speak to them without any words. They will be won over [2] by observing your pure and reverent lives. (1 Peter 3:1 NLT)

Children Should Obey and Honour Their Parents
Journal Entry   **29 November 2019**
Blog Entry   **29 November 2019**

Children, obey your parents because you belong to the Lord, for this is the right thing to do. [2] "Honour your father and mother." This is the first commandment with a promise: [3] If you honour your father and mother, "things will go well for you, and you will have a long life on the earth." (Ephesians 6:1-3 NLT)

Looks like I wrote very little on this topic back in April 2015 when I was going through Ephesians. All I had to say at the time was that children should honour and obey their parents even if the parent seems unfair.

An interesting point here that I missed back then was that this command from God comes with a promise. If you honour your father and mother, "things will go well for you, and you will have a long life on earth." So, this is a promise from God, and God can be trusted to keep His promises!

I must admit that I've struggled with this one, as I am sure other children have who lived in abusive homes. How can you honour your parent when they are doing things that hurt you or other people? No child should ever stay in an abusive situation. Period. Given that, when the child grows up and is no longer under the power of that parent, working out how to honour a parent who didn't act the way a parent should is still a tough road.

I don't have any answers or useful insight on this one. I found it very difficult to honour my parents, particularly my dad. I am just glad my children have grown up in an environment that allows them to honour their parents without struggling through the pain of emotional baggage.

The Whole Armour of God
Journal Entry   2 December 2019
Blog Entry   2 December 2019

Wrapping up my blog on Ephesians today with Ephesians 6:10-20. Didn't write about this in 2015 when I was going through the Bible. Perhaps it was because I knew this scripture well, so nothing stuck out for me to write about. However, in recent weeks I've heard the Lord telling me to pray every morning for spiritual protection, that my God would fight the battles in the spiritual realm for me so that I can truly live the abundant life He has planned for me. I felt that I wasn't asking for help, and by not asking, I was actually trying to do things in my own power. The Father was reminding me that I can't do it alone and that I need a fresh anointing of His power every morning.

We Need Help in this Life to Fight the Battles We Can't See

The important point here is that while we are living here on earth, there are two worlds at work in our lives. There is the temporal world (the one we can see, feel, and touch), but the spiritual world is also at work in our lives. We can't see it, so most of us don't even realize there is anything more going on in our lives beyond the things we are able to see.

However, the spiritual forces are very real and powerful entities that are shaping and moving us and the things in our lives. When Jesus died on the cross, He opened up the door that allows us to directly ask for God's help in fighting the battles in the spiritual world. These are battles that we aren't able to fight for ourselves. All we need to do is ask for help and put our trust in God to fight on our behalf.

Our Spiritual Armour
Stand your ground, putting on the belt of truth and the body armour of God's righteousness. (Ephesians 6:14 NLT)

The Belt of Truth and the Body Armour of God's Righteousness: depend on God's word to know the truth of what is right and wrong and stay grounded in the truth. Don't let the culture fool you into believing things are good and right if they are inconsistent with God's word. It can get very confusing out there, but if you stay grounded in what God's word says you'll always have the right moral compass. Also, refuse to receive any condemnation that tells you that you aren't good enough, or valuable. This is a lie from the pit of hell. You are unique, important, and were created for a great purpose in this world!

For shoes, put on the peace that comes from the Good News so that you will be fully prepared. (Ephesians 6:15 NLT)

The Shoes of Peace: peace that comes with the Good News. Don't be overwhelmed with worry. Instead, remain in the peace that comes from knowing that whatever happens, you are loved by your creator, and He is for you not against you.

In addition to all of these, hold up the shield of faith to stop the fiery arrows of the devil. (Ephesians 6:16 NLT)

The Shield of Faith is meant to stop the fiery arrows of the devil. Whenever you begin to doubt the realness of God, or things come into your life that frighten or upset you, hold tight to your faith in God. Remember that He sent his one and only son Jesus, who loved you so much that he gave up His life for you. No matter what happens in life, hold on to your faith in Him. No one can ever take that away from you! This is a personal gift from Almighty God to you.

Put on salvation as your helmet, and take the sword of the Spirit, which is the word of God. (Ephesians 6:17 NLT)

Salvation as your helmet: protect your mind with a helmet of salvation knowing that you belong to God, that He paid a high price for you because He loves you so much. You are saved and safe in His loving arms at all times.

The Sword of the Spirit, which is the word of God: the more you know God's word, which is the Bible, the better you can use this sword. When circumstances in life come along, you can use the word to help you fight through. You can use scripture to help you understand, cope, and conquer all circumstances.

[10] A final word: Be strong in the Lord and in his mighty power. [11] Put on all of God's armour so that you will be able to stand firm against all strategies of the devil. [12] For we are not fighting against flesh-and-blood enemies, but against evil rulers and authorities of the unseen world, against mighty powers in this dark world, and against evil spirits in the heavenly places.
(Ephesians 6:10-12 NLT)

WINTER

8
PAUL'S LETTER TO THE CHURCH IN PHILIPPI

God's Work Continues Through the Philippians and Through Paul
Journal Entry   30 April 2015
Blog Entry   5 December 2019

Paul's letter to the Philippians is sometimes called the "Joy" letter. The concept of joyfulness or rejoicing is mentioned 16 times in this short letter. The church in Philippi had brought Paul so much encouragement that he wrote them this letter to express his love and affection for them and to encourage them to keep making progress in their faith. Though they were already doing quite well, Paul tells them not to stop there and rest but to keep moving forward in their faith by practicing the virtues of love and service to others. The church in Philippi was the first church Paul had founded in Europe, and the first convert was Lydia.

And I am certain that God, who began the good work within you, will continue his work until it is finally finished on the day when Christ Jesus returns. (Philippians 1:6 NLT)

I love this verse as it gives me encouragement for each day that God won't give up on me. He will continue to move in my life so I can go deeper in understanding and in learning to carry out His purpose for me in the world.

No Matter the Motive, the Gospel Message is the Same

In Philippians 1:12-18, Paul talks about the Good News being preached where he is being held as a prisoner. Paul tells them that some people are preaching the Good News with sincere motives, but some are preaching it just to get him into more trouble. However, Paul states that even if it is preached based on wrong motives, he is still happy it is preached, and the message of Jesus is getting out there. This spoke to me as I often think that I don't do enough for the Kingdom or spread the Gospel message properly, particularly in my mission field at the office. This passage gives me assurances that whatever way the message gets out there, the most important thing is that it does get out! Praise you, God, for your encouragement to me this morning!

Update - 4 December 2019

For you have been given not only the privilege of trusting in Christ but also the privilege of suffering for him. (Philippians 1:29 NLT)

As I was writing my blog today, this verse jumped off the page for me. I looked up some commentary on it, and generally, I've found it to be about the idea that believing and suffering are both parts of the life of a Christ-follower. Suffering is a gift from God, just as faith is a gift from God. This certainly is a little hard to digest at first. I think many of us fall into the myth of thinking that if we believe in Jesus, we will avoid suffering. However, this just isn't true. Then again, suffering with no purpose is not what Paul is talking about here either. He is telling the

Philippians that suffering because of your faith in Christ is all part of being a Christian.

Be Humble and Wait for God to Promote You
Journal Entry   2 May 2015
Blog Entry   6 December 2019

"Don't be selfish, don't try to impress others. Be humble thinking of others as better than yourself. Don't look out only for your own interests but take an interest in others too."
(Philippians 2:3-4 NLT)

I had not actually written any notes for this one back in 2015. I just copied these two verses out. When I read it today, what struck me was the idea of humbling ourselves instead of promoting ourselves—waiting with a humble, obedient, and thankful heart for God to promote us. This is a difficult thing to do when God doesn't seem to be doing things according to our timetable, yet this is what Paul instructs us to do. We should work hard, not be lazy, and try to accomplish things in this life. However, if things aren't working out the way he had hoped, at the speed we had hoped they would happen, we need to be patient and wait for God to work in our situation.

As Christ's Followers, We Must Have the Same Attitude He Had

6 Though he was God,
  he did not think of equality with God
  as something to cling to.
7 Instead, he gave up his divine privileges;
  he took the humble position of a slave
  and was born as a human being.
When he appeared in human form,
8 he humbled himself in obedience to God
  and died a criminal's death on a cross.
9 Therefore, God elevated him to the place of highest honour

and gave him the name above all other names,
¹⁰ that at the name of Jesus every knee should bow,
  in heaven and on earth and under the earth,
¹¹ and every tongue declare that Jesus Christ is Lord,
  to the glory of God the Father.
(Philippians 2:6-11 NLT)

God is Working in You
***Journal Entry**   5 May 2015*
***Blog Entry**   9 December 2019*

For God is working in you, giving you the desire and the power to do what pleases him. (Philippians 2:13 NLT)

I've been mulling over 2:13 in my mind the last few days, and I find it very inspiring that God will work in me and give me the desire and the power to do what pleases Him. I find this to be so true as I constantly feel called to do the right thing. To eat properly, to exercise, to treat others right, not to use bad language, I could go on and on. Sometimes, actually often, I feel guilty for not doing all that I should or all that I feel God creating the desire in me to do. But I know that guilt doesn't come from the Lord. I need to press on in faith and rely on the power God will provide for me to accomplish the desires He has created in me to do.

...For God's way of making us right with himself depends on faith. (Philippians 3:9 NLT)

We are made right through faith. Faith is the key! The key that unlocks our lives and allows us to be free to be all that God created us to be.

Philippians - The Letter of Joy and Encouragement
***Journal Entry**   9 May 2015*
***Blog Entry**   13 December 2019*

In many of the study materials I read, it states that Philippians is the "Joy" book. For me, it's more the "Encouragement" book. I wrote down a few key scripture verses from Philippians that encourage me:

And I am certain that God, who began the good work within you, will continue his work until it is finally finished on the day when Christ Jesus returns. (Philippians 1:6 NLT)

God will bring to completion the great work He has begun in me! He has anointed me, called me to Himself, by His Holy Spirit. He is teaching me day by day, shaping me moment by moment, to be the creation He planned and created me to be. My part is to co-operate with His leading. I do this by listening to and obeying that still, small voice that helps me make the right decisions.

For God is working in you, giving you the desire and the power to do what pleases him. (Philippians 2:13 NLT)

God creates the desire in me to do the things I should do in life and then gives me the power to carry it through. So how do I hear from God? I just continue to focus on having faith!

...For God's way of making us right with himself depends on faith. (Philippians 3:9 NLT)

It is such an amazing supernatural phenomenon, but as long as I keep putting God first and at the front of my mind, I have more peace, and other things in life just fall into place. Not that I don't have to put effort into it. I guess that's the difference for me in the new awakening I am experiencing, in this new closeness with God. I feel it is linked to my willingness to participate with God, to commit to doing some things I hear the Holy Spirit calling me to do. One of them is getting up a little early each day to spend time with God first thing in the morning. The other is to give up overeating and to have discipline in my eating and exercising. Also, to focus on "lovely" things.

I don't mean to say that I have already achieved these things or that I have already reached perfection. But I press on to possess that perfection for which Christ Jesus first possessed me. [13] No, dear brothers and sisters, I have not achieved it, but I focus on this one thing: Forgetting the past and looking forward to what lies ahead, [14] I press on to reach the end of the race and receive the heavenly prize for which God, through Christ Jesus, is calling us.
(Philippians 3:12-14 NLT)

As Paul says, it is not that I have already arrived, but I keep pressing on toward the goal! I hold on to the progress I have made. I'm not going to be perfect every day, but they key is not to give up! Keep on pressing in and pressing on. Get back up and keep going. Don't think of it as failing and starting over. Just think of it as part of the process, and keep going, keep pressing on.

Fix your thoughts on what is true, and honourable, and right, and pure, and lovely, and admirable. Think about things that are excellent and worthy of praise. (Philippians 4:8 NLT)

Focus on lovely things, things that are honourable and true. Shifting my focus in this way makes me feel more joy, and pulls me closer to God, allowing me to have a stronger sense of His presence. It is important in this world and culture that is so filled with wickedness and vile profane garbage to keep our eyes fixed on what is good and true. When bad thoughts start filling my mind, I catch them and throw them out in Jesus' name.

9
PAUL'S LETTER TO THE CHURCH IN COLOSSAE

Jesus is the Visible Image of Our Creator - Whether We Choose to Believe it or Not Doesn't Change that Fact
Journal Entry   13 May 2015
Blog Entry   16 December 2019

Christ is the visible image of the invisible God.
He existed before anything was created and is supreme over all creation,^{16} for through him God created everything
in the heavenly realms and on earth.
He made the things we can see
  and the things we can't see—
such as thrones, kingdoms, rulers, and authorities in the unseen world. Everything was created through him and for him.
(Colossians 1:15-16 NLT*)*

It came forcefully to me that Jesus isn't an "add-on" that we can choose to accept or reject as part of our lives. He is the Almighty Creator of life! Our Creator chose to create everything through Him and for Him, so He is the beginning and the end, the fullness of all life.

Jesus is Much Bigger Than We Realize
He's our everything, and is intimately woven through everything. We can't choose to reject Him because that would mean we reject our world and our own lives. He's much bigger than we understand Him to be. We somehow have missed this whole beginning and end part of His deity. We see Jesus as someone we can choose to follow or reject, but He is in our lives and in everything in the world and in the Heavenly realm.

What is Our Choice, Then?
The choice we have is to acknowledge and receive His love and friendship as we journey through this life and world He has created for us, or to attempt to live in His world independently and ignore Him. No matter what we choose, with Him or without Him, it is still His world, created in and through Him.

Dear Lord Jesus, forgive me for not honouring you as I should. Help me to live every second of every day acknowledging you and your Lordship over my life!

You've Been Set Free, So Stay Free
Journal Entry   19 May 2015
Blog Entry   18 December 2019

Paul tells us not to "drift" away from the assurance, the belief, that Christ by dying on the cross has reconciled us to Himself. To stand firm, stand firm in the knowledge that you are His, that He died to set you free.

But you must continue to believe this truth and stand firmly in it. Don't drift away from the assurance you received when you heard the Good News. (Colossians 1:23 NLT)

As Paul said in Galatians 5:1 – don't live as a slave, stay free! You've been set free. Live as you are free. Don't let the oppression of sin and the enemy smother you and hold you back. Christ gave everything He had so that you could live an amazing life, don't waste His gift to you by drifting back into your old ways, into sinful ways. You don't need to give into that. You can remain free; all the work has been done for you. You just have to live it out!

And the Secret is This, Christ Lives in You
Journal Entry   21 May 2015
Blog Entry   20 December 2019

"And the secret is this, Christ lives in you"
(Colossians 1:27 NLT)

Just prior to this statement, Paul talks about the "secret" that was hidden from human understanding but is now revealed, and the secret is that we have Christ living in us!

Let His Light Shine Out Through You

Lately for me, I've been praying to let Him live out through me. I don't want to bury Him in me. I feel like that happens when there is too much of me and not enough of Him showing on the outside! He lives in all of us, but it's our choice to acknowledge Him, believe in Him, and trust Him with our lives or allow Him to live through us. This is how we become God's Church in the world. The more we allow Him to live out through our actions and lives, the more fruit of the Spirit we will experience in our own lives, and the more truly satisfying our lives will be.

My prayer is that there will be more of Him and less of me showing on the outside and ruling my thoughts and mind. I give you control, Jesus. Use my life for Your purpose and Your glory, whatever that is, because Your plan is good and true and much better than what I, a mere human, could ever do or think. I don't want to waste this one life I have. I want to live it for Your glory and purpose so that when I get back home to heaven, I can hear You say, "well done!"

[25] God has given me the responsibility of serving his church by proclaiming his entire message to you. [26] This message was kept secret for centuries and generations past, but now it has been revealed to God's people. [27] For God wanted them to know that the riches and glory of Christ are for you Gentiles, too. And this is the secret: Christ lives in you. This gives you assurance of sharing his glory.
(Colossians 1:25-27 NLT)

Let Your Roots Grow Deep in Christ
Journal Entry   21 May 2015
Blog Entry   23 December 2019

Let your roots grow deep in Christ (Colossians 2:7 NLT)

I recognize this from one of the other letters, Ephesians 3:17. I believe our roots grow deep by studying the Word, prayer, and living our lives by letting Christ live out through us and being obedient to the whisper of the Holy Spirit. As our experiences allow us to trust Christ with our lives, we become more rooted in Him. Like a strong, old tree, it becomes very difficult to pull us out of the relationship with Him. We grow deeper and deeper in Him, in our relationship and understanding of Him, and as we do, our faith becomes stronger and stronger, and our understanding becomes clearer and clearer. We start off as a little sapling that can get pulled up, but as we grow in Him, we become stronger and are able to withstand the wind (our culture and people) from bouncing us around. We eventually get to the point where our trunk is so solid that we can just enjoy the breeze and not be shaken.

Update - 28 May 2017

As I'm typing this up from my notes, I'm thinking of some of the trees in our backyard that are huge and have very deep roots. In the winter storms, sometimes big branches will break off and fall to the ground, leaving a scar on the tree, but the tree survives, and its foundation and roots are still intact and giving life to the tree. I see that as a visual of some of the hard things we have to deal with in our lives. These challenging times might break us a bit, and we might lose some of our innocence or maybe even trust, but we can continue to grow new branches because our roots are in solid ground. Though these events may have broken us, they didn't destroy us!

This reminds me of one of my favourite scriptures in 2nd Corinthians.

[8] We are pressed on every side by troubles, but we are not crushed. We are perplexed, but not driven to despair. [9] We are hunted down, but never abandoned by God. We get knocked down, but we are not destroyed. (2nd Corinthians 4:8-9 NLT)

10
PAUL'S FIRST AND SECOND LETTERS TO TIMOTHY

Conduct of Elders and Deacons
Journal Entry   30 May 2015
Blog Entry   27 December 2019

1st Timothy 3 describes appropriate behaviour for elders and deacons in the church. Paul tells Timothy that this is a great responsibility, and a man's conduct must be without reproach if he is chosen to serve in this capacity. He must be a man who treats his wife and children well, s man whose children respect and obey him, a man who conducts himself well and doesn't drink too much.

Paul goes on to say that "new" believers shouldn't be put in the position of elders or deacons as they will likely become prideful. One must have some experience living with God in their life before being placed in a position of authority in the church.

My Life Application Bible Study Notes refer to 2nd Timothy 2:2, wherein Paul explains that followers of Jesus can be teachers in everyday relationships with people that cross their paths. Paul states that it is important that these everyday teachers also adhere to the guidelines provided for leaders, elders, and deacons. Since they are bringing the Gospel to others or trying to show them Christ, their behaviour should be the same as that which the deacons and elders are called to.

My two cents: I would think this is the preferred model of spreading the Gospel, but not the only model.

Paul described in his letter to the Philippians that some who were holding him prisoner were teaching the Gospel, not in the best way, but at least Christ was being preached! I don't think anyone should ever feel unqualified to spread the Good News of the Gospel. I think the point Paul was making here was that church leaders and teachers, those in a position of authority in the church, are called to a higher standard of personal conduct.

Those others do not have pure motives as they preach about Christ. They preach with selfish ambition, not sincerely, intending to make my chains more painful to me. ^{18} But that doesn't matter. Whether their motives are false or genuine, the message about Christ is being preached either way, so I rejoice. And I will continue to rejoice. (Philippians 1:17-18 NLT)

He is Always Present
Journal Entry   30 May 2015
Blog Entry   30 December 2019

He is present with me, over every detail of my life. I was on Highway 417 and had a strong message to drive the speed limit. I never do that – I always drive a little faster. I almost passed someone, but felt such a strong call not to, so I thought this was God protecting me from something, maybe an accident. Then, a little further down the highway, there was a speed trap! I laughed hilariously in the car and thanked God for watching over me.

I learned through that experience a new level of the reality of God in my life. This is an answer to prayer. I prayed recently that I would know God better, see Him more clearly, not just as a distant God. I feel that there's a barrier I need to break through to really let my guard down or to expunge all doubt from my mind that God is God! Really our Creator, really who the Bible says He is and not just a myth.

The Maple Keys
Journal Entry   30 May 2015

Blog Entry   3 January 2020

This is the second personal blog entry for this same day. I had another revelation from the Holy Spirit, and it was a strong message, so I wanted to share it.

"Another revelation I had just yesterday (May 29, 2015) came from my view of the thousands of Maple Keys *(seeds that fall from Maple trees)* outside covering the driveway, grass, rooftops, and roads. I was walking out to the car and was struck by the thousands and thousands of Maple Keys scattered everywhere. I thought that there certainly need to be a lot of Maple Keys for even a few trees to grow. Then the Holy Spirit revealed to me, or comforted me, with the thought that even though some of the seeds scattered may not grow into trees, it is still necessary to scatter them.

Keep Sowing

I felt the Holy Spirit was telling me not to be discouraged if not every seed of faith I scatter seems to be worth it, or doesn't seem to be growing into fruition. I should continue to scatter many seeds, as I don't know which ones will take root. I felt God was telling me not to be discouraged, but to keep scattering those seeds.

Striving for Money
Journal Entry   3 June 2015
Blog Entry   6 January 2020

Yet true godliness with contentment is itself great wealth. [7] After all, we brought nothing with us when we came into the world, and we can't take anything with us when we leave it. [8] So if we have enough food and clothing, let us be content. (1st Timothy 6:6-8 NLT)

Striving for money, should not be our focus. If we have extra money after our own needs are met, we should help others. This passage about money was very comforting to me today as we currently have quite a lot of debt, and sometimes I worry about it and wish we had more money. However, we manage to pay our bills, and I know someday we'll have it all paid up. I sometimes think God holds us in this state, having just enough from week to week, so we will continue to rely on Him and trust Him and not ourselves. Thank you, God, that you have always provided us with enough to be very comfortable.

Update - 15 July 2017

Another testament to God looking after us. My husband retired from full-time work last November, and I just retired this past April. We are adjusting to our new income level in retirement. God has more than provided for us as we both have great pensions, and we are so thankful for that. However, we still have quite a large debt load, two kids at home, still to go through post-secondary school, and each month we have just enough to cover everything.

I was committed to tithing 10% this year. I had tried to tithe for the past seven or eight years, but I always ended up being a bit short and dipping into my tithing money to cover other things. But this year, since we had severance pay invested as a cushion, I had committed to tithe consistently and take money out of the severance investments if we fell too far behind. We had been using some of that severance to the point that I didn't want to use any more of it in case we had some big emergency that we needed to cover. We were almost maxed out on our credit cards, so a large expense would have been complicated to resolve. I realized that I had to stop dipping into the severance money, I resolved that we should do our best not to dip into that money, but I was also resolved to keep tithing. We had twelve days to go until payday, and money was definitely getting scarce since we had had 3, rather than the usual 2, mortgage payments coming out for that month.

Then guess what God did? Completely out of the blue, my husband was asked if he would consider cleaning the church while the regular custodian was on holiday. My husband agreed to do it to help out and then found out they were going to pay him for it! Incredible that God provided in this way. Completely unexpected, God reached down and put this plan into motion.

⁹ But people who long to be rich fall into temptation and are trapped by many foolish and harmful desires that plunge them into ruin and destruction. ¹⁰ For the love of money is the root of all kinds of evil. And some people, craving money, have wandered from the true faith and pierced themselves with many sorrows. (1st Timothy 6:9-10 NLT)

Better to love God than to love money.

Teach These Truths
Journal Entry 8 June 2015
Blog Entry 9 January 2020

"You have heard me teach things that have been confirmed by many reliable witnesses. Now teach these truths to other worthy people who will be able to pass them on to others." (2nd Timothy 2:2 NLT)

This passage stuck out to me today. At first, I thought it meant not to waste our time teaching or passing the Gospel along to people who don't want to hear it. Similar to the *"shake the dust off your shoes from the villages that don't receive you" passages; Matthew 10:14, Mark 6:11, and Luke 9:5.* I feel that this gives me the excuse not to try and reach people who aren't open to hearing the Good News about Jesus. But I struggle with that sometimes. I worry about who's going to reach them. However, I received a realization today that maybe God is trying to reign me in a bit and let me know that it's not up to me. It's up to Him who gets reached, by whom, and when! There's a tension there for me. I am realizing that maybe I'm too arrogant in thinking it's me that needs to reach everyone. I need to remember it's not about me; it's all about Him. I need to only do what I hear Him calling me to do.

The other thought I had about this scripture was that telling the wrong people at the wrong time could even do damage to the Kingdom. It could give the enemy tools to work with. On the one side, I want to be sure I fulfil my responsibility to reach the world with the Good News, but I don't want to be overzealous and run ahead of God and perhaps cause damage. I need to be still, listen closely, walk closely, and stay in step with God. If I do this, I will know when and where to speak up or to hold my tongue.

Stay Focused and Soldier On
Journal Entry   8 June 2015
Blog Entry   10 January 2020

Endure suffering along with me, as a good soldier of Christ Jesus. ⁴ Soldiers don't get tied up in the affairs of civilian life, for then they cannot please the officer who enlisted them. ⁵ And athletes cannot win the prize unless they follow the rules. ⁶ And hardworking farmers should be the first to enjoy the fruit of their labour. ⁷ Think about what I am saying. The Lord will help you understand all these things. (2nd Timothy 2:3-7 NLT)

This passage in Timothy also stood out to me today in that we must not get caught up in the world or in the petty things in life. We need to stay focused on the things of God, the things of eternity. Similar to dying to self and living in this new life. We must continue to keep ourselves above all that noise so that we can hear and see God.

How do we do this? We need to continue to refresh ourselves with the power of the Holy Spirit and not rely on ourselves but fully rely on God. We need to realize and embrace that He is our source of peace and our source of power, our source of everything!

Update - 15 July 2017

A song I love to listen to when I'm exercising is "Oceans", by Hillsong. One line in particular is about "keeping my eyes above the waves". I feel that this is the same theme as 2nd Timothy 2:3-7. This is particularly useful for me to remember as I deal with some difficult family situations. When my emotions start to flare up, I remind myself of that line from the song, stop sinking, and keep my eyes above the waves!

Battling Doubt and Arrogance

Even though I know in my heart the above is true, that I am absolutely nothing without God, and that I continually rely on God for everything and see Him working amazing things in my life; my flesh keeps telling me, or the enemy keeps telling me, that I'm doing all of this myself, that I'm really great and don't really need God that much. This seed of doubt keeps floating around in my head and heart. Ahhhh, it's such a struggle! I feel like pride, or something is just blocking me from completely acknowledging to myself that God does every single thing for me. Maybe it comes from growing up in a chaotic home with abuse and alcoholism. Maybe I learned to rely on myself so heavily and not trust anyone that I am having trouble completely trusting God. I tell other people testimony stories about the amazing things God has done in my life, but I sometimes have trouble completely accepting them in my own soul. Dear Lord God, please change my heart, my mind, my everything so that I can completely be the person you want me to be in this world, to walk the path you have for me to walk, and to achieve the things you have for me to achieve. Please help me bring You glory and give You the glory! Teach me how to completely trust You and give You all the Glory. Help my life be all about

You.

Being Ready to Do God's Work
Journal Entry   8 June 2015
Blog Entry   13 January 2020

In a rich person's home there are gold and silver utensils and there are clay utensils. The expensive utensils are used for special occasions and the cheap ones for everyday use. If you keep yourself pure, you will be a special utensil for honourable use. Your life will be clean and you will be ready for the Master to use you for every good work. (2Timothy 2:20-21 NLT)

That's what I want to be, ready for God to use in special honourable circumstances. Maybe that motivation is selfish because I want to do amazing, jaw-dropping, miraculous things! However, if I'm completely honest, I want to do these things to bring glory and honour to my family and me and not only to God. Dear God, help me rid myself of every wrong motivation or intention so I can be used by you in the world to glorify YOU! Not to bring glory to me. Help me learn how to do that. Amen.

My Dad died five months ago, and God just dropped into my heart while I was getting ready for work that He gave me the special mission of being with Dad when he died because I was ready for that task. He chose me for that purpose. Thank you, God!

Update - 15 July 2017

I just reread the notes I had written about the night my dad died. I was with him alone during his final hours, and it was a unique time in my life. I wanted to remember every detail, so I wrote about it shortly afterward.

To be honest, in reflecting on the notes, I think God gave

me that mission because He wanted to show me that I am imperfect, I am fallible, and if He is not helping me, I can't do the things I need to do in this life. Looking back on it now, I think God has been teaching me a lot about my own pride and arrogance and self-righteousness over the past two years but particularly since I retired. Thank you, God, for teaching me these lessons so gently, I am afraid of learning them harshly, and you know that, of course. Thank you that I don't have to be afraid to learn, that you love me, and whatever you do in my life is for my good and to bring glory to You!

Handling Strife
Journal Entry   10 June 2015
Blog Entry   15 January 2020

Don't get involved in foolish ignorant arguments that only start fights. A servant of the Lord must not quarrel but must be kind to everyone, be able to teach, and be patient with difficult people.
(2nd Timothy 2:23-24 NLT)

Whew, that's a mouthful! I've found that I can easily get caught up in arguments with family members. They often judge each other's motives and quarrel, and it is so easy for me to fall into those situations by siding with one family member or another. I realize, from this scripture, that as a servant of the Lord, I need to rise above the din of those petty quarrels and stay true to God by having patience and pursuing peace with everyone. Paul instructs us that in our new life in Christ this is how we are to behave in such circumstances. I believe I have often been the peacemaker in these cases, but I admit that in the past, I have fallen into the pit sometimes and have been down there slinging the mud. With your help Lord, I will stay above the din, be the peacemaker, and be patient and kind with everyone. Please help me to recognize when I need to be silent, and when to talk. When I do talk, please give me wisdom, so my words will not provoke further strife but will be the wise counsel that calms.

Update - 15 July 2017

The Lord is so amazing! I just happened to be typing these particular notes up at a time when I really needed to be reminded of them! My Step-Mother passed away a few weeks ago, and we are currently in the throes of going through Dad's house and all their belongings. One of my sisters is the executor and power of attorney, so she has taken everything in hand. My brother and I are on the periphery. There has been quite a lot of dissension between the three of us in the past, so it is difficult to go through this process. However, God is teaching me how to remain silent and keep my emotions in check. It's not easy, but with God's help, I know that it will go better than I could have done on my own. In these situations, I need to realize that God is so present and moving so much. If it weren't for God and my obedience to His call, I would not be handling any of this well. I would not have the peace that I have. My old self would not be behaving the way my new self in Christ is behaving in all of this!

Thank you, Jesus, for dying so that I can have this new life and new peace in every part of my life. Thank you for allowing me to chip away and breakthrough to see and acknowledge the details you are working out in my life!

You Will be Persecuted
Journal Entry   11 June 2015
Blog Entry   18 January 2020

You should know this, Timothy, that in the last days there will be very difficult times. ² For people will love only themselves and their money. They will be boastful and proud, scoffing at God, disobedient to their parents, and ungrateful. They will consider nothing sacred. ³ They will be unloving and unforgiving; they will slander

others and have no self-control. They will be cruel and hate what is good. ⁴ They will betray their friends, be reckless, be puffed up with pride, and love pleasure rather than God. (2nd Timothy 3:1-4 NLT)
¹² Yes, and everyone who wants to live a godly life in Christ Jesus will suffer persecution. ¹³ But evil people and impostors will flourish. They will deceive others and will themselves be deceived. "And everyone who wants to live a Godly life in Christ will suffer persecution"
(2nd Timothy 3:12-13 NLT)

So, way back over 2000 years ago, Paul predicted this would be the case. Doesn't this sound exactly like the world we live in today? Paul told us that we would be persecuted and scoffed at by some and thought to be naive or misled by others if we chose to follow the path of Christ and trust faithfully in God. But hold fast to the truth, don't give up what you know to be true. Following the teachings of Christ and of the Bible is the right way, and the only way to experience real truth. You know this in your soul, so don't worry when persecution comes your way.

⁴ Little children (believers, dear ones), you are of God and you belong to Him and have [already] overcome them [the agents of the antichrist]; because He who is in you is greater than he (Satan) who is in the world [of sinful mankind]. ⁵ They [who teach twisted doctrine] are of the world and belong to it; therefore they speak from the [viewpoint of the] world [with its immoral freedom and baseless theories—demanding compliance with their opinions and ridiculing the values of the upright], and the [gullible one of the] world listens closely and pays attention to them. ⁶ We [who teach God's word] are from God [energized by the Holy Spirit], and whoever knows God [through personal experience] listens to us [and has a deeper understanding of Him]. Whoever is not of God does not listen to us. By this we know [without any doubt] the spirit of truth [motivated by God] and the spirit of error [motivated by Satan]. (1 John 4:4-6 AMP)

Receive the Supernatural Life Reading Scripture Brings
Journal Entry   15 June 2015
Blog Entry   20 January 2020

All scripture is inspired by God and is useful to teach us what is TRUE to make us realize what is wrong in our lives. It corrects us when we are wrong and teaches us to do what is right. God uses it to prepare His people to do every good work.
(2 Timothy 3:16-17 NLT)

This passage is so helpful to me today! I've been feeling a little down and lost these past few days, having gotten caught up in the worries of the world and taken my focus off of the Lord. This scripture reminds me to get my mind back in the His Word, to keep my life on track and in balance, to get the proper perspective back.

Don't Fall into Doom and Gloom Thinking of the Enemy

The enemy tries to lead me away into negative thinking of doom and gloom, but the Word works in my spirit and brings a ray of sunshine into my soul, reminding me of what is true and good and worthwhile. Simply reading the word this morning has supernaturally blown new life and optimism into my soul, refreshed me, and lifted my spirit.

The statements Paul makes in 2nd Tim 3:16-17 are stating something, offering information and teaching, and at the same time, what I am reading is actually manifesting itself in me! Quite amazing!

Lord, help me see more of you and your miracles in my life. Open my heart to the many wonderful things you are doing in my life. Don't let me miss them. Thank you, Lord, for rejuvenating the truth for me this morning through my reading of your word. Thank you for drawing so close to me every time I make an effort to draw close to you. Thank you for reassuring me of your realness and faithfulness today as I experience your touch on me this morning!

Something else that popped out for me from the passage this morning was verse 17. I've often heard verse 16, am familiar with that part, but verse 17 tells us that God uses His word to prepare His people to do good works. So again, the word is not only something we read; when we read it, it comes alive and infuses us with the power to do the things we are called to do. It's a mystery beyond our understanding how this happens, but it does happen. It just happened to me! Our outlook, our heart, confidence, and optimism are boosted, and our minds begin to think in a new direction and on the things God is calling us to do. Praise God for all He is, has done, and is doing! Amen.

11
THE BOOK OF HEBREWS

Jesus is Not Ashamed to Call Us His Brothers and Sisters
Journal Entry   19 June 2015
Blog Entry   22 January 2020

God, for whom and through whom everything was made, chose to bring many children into glory. And it was only right that he should make Jesus, through his suffering, a perfect leader, fit to bring them into their salvation. ¹¹ So now Jesus and the ones he makes holy have the same Father. That is why Jesus is not ashamed to call them his brothers and sisters. (Hebrews 2:10-11 NLT)

I don't feel worthy to call Jesus my brother, but here it says that He calls me His sister. That He is with us as close to us as a brother, our perfect leader. We, who accept Him as our Saviour, belong to His little group, His adopted family. He cares for us, helps us, and leads us as we journey through our lives. He's our big brother who knows the way and helps us fight our battles and make wise decisions.

Lord Jesus, help me remember to lean on you and trust you as a wise and powerful older brother, who only has my best interests at heart and who would give His life for me. Help me recognize who you are to me.

Promised Rest for God's People
Journal Entry   22 June 2015
Blog Entry   25 January 2020

Hebrews 4 and the end of chapter 3 talk about entering God's rest. When I first read it, it immediately struck me that this rest is synonymous with the peace that surpasses all understanding referred to in Philippians 4:6-7.

⁶ Don't worry about anything; instead, pray about everything. Tell God what you need, and thank him for all he has done. ⁷ Then you will experience God's peace, which exceeds anything we can understand. His peace will guard your hearts and minds as you live in Christ Jesus. (Philippians 4:6-7 NLT)

A secondary thought led me to think of it as heaven or the afterlife. Of course, they are both God's rest, but we don't have to wait to die to enter God's rest. God's rest can begin as soon as we are willing to turn our lives over to Him, to draw near to Him, and to make time for a relationship with Him! I've found this to be true in my life. The more I fill my life with God, the more peaceful I become.

How to Find Peace
So, you might wonder how to get to this place of peace. I've found that taking regular time out to read the Bible and to pray, to seek God out, to trust Him, to pray in every situation, to make Him the centre on which you base all decisions, is a good road map to this peace. When you do those things, you end up living and breathing God in every moment of your life, and peace is the by-product!

Update - 27 July 2017

As I write this up, I'm thinking that the above might seem like a tall order, particularly for folks who don't really have any kind of relationship with God. However, you can just start out small, start out praying about one decision. Then read the word for a few minutes every second day. After that, it just grows and grows until you reach the point where you are always consulting God on every decision, thinking about Him when you wake up and when you go to sleep. He starts to consume your thoughts, and the more He does, the more peace you have.

Your spiritual enemy will try to tell you this is too hard, too confusing, and is dumb, but don't listen to him. He's a liar and a thief who is out to steal the joy from your life, John 10:10. Talk back to him and tell him that you won't listen to his lies.

^{19} Behold, I have given you authority to tread on serpents and scorpions, and over all the power of the enemy, and nothing shall hurt you. (Luke 10:19 ESV)

You have been given the power to defeat your spiritual enemy. That is why Christ suffered and died so that you wouldn't have to believe those lies and fall under (your spiritual enemy) the Devil's authority anymore. Refuse to listen to him and trust (have faith) in God, your heavenly father who loves you!

Hebrews mentions several times not to "harden your hearts" toward God. As situations come up in life, choose to react or behave in the way you know God is calling you to, and your life will be filled with God's peace.

Keep Pressing in to Learn More, and Don't Fall Away
Journal Entry   25 June 2015
Blog Entry   28 January 2020

The passage, starting in Hebrews 5:11 to 6:12, is a call to spiritual growth. The author is telling us that we need to grow spiritually, not just stay in the basics of faith forever. He also tells us not to learn just the basics, practise that for a little while, and then reject God and move on to something else, or fall back into our old ways. We should continually be learning more about God, more about how we can live our lives every day under the cover of God's love and the Holy Spirit's direction.

It's Easier to Give Up and Slip Away

I know that it is so easy to fall away and not stay close to God. It's like our natural state is away from God, so we have to make an effort every day, or even several times a day, to remember who we are in Christ, to remember that we are God's sons and daughters! He is our Father, our Creator. I find that I need to remind myself of that every day and even several times during the day. I think maybe this is what the scripture about renewing your mind is talking about.

Do not conform to the pattern of this world, but be transformed by the renewing of your mind. Then you will be able to test and approve what God's will is—his good, pleasing and perfect will.
(Romans 12:2 NLT)

Keep refreshing your mind and your spirit, and remind yourself of who you are in Christ! Remember that the Holy Spirit is guiding and directing you and that your Father God has promised to work all things out for your good because He loves you so much.

Pray for God's Help to Stay in Step with Him

How do you do this? How do you stop from slipping away? You just ask God to renew your mind, to refresh your spirit. You can't do it by yourself, you need His help, and He will help you, but you have to ask Him. I know it sounds strange and is counter to this world's ways, but it is truth! He will help you if you continue to ask for His help. One day you'll look back, and you'll see how your life has changed and how God is playing a big role in your life. Don't fall back. Don't slip away. Keep making the effort to stay close to God.

In my life Application Bible study notes, it says that as we put into practice what we learn about the life God wants us to live, our capacity to understand will grow. I believe this is so true. I feel words aren't adequate to explain it, but I've found that the more I try to live the life God wants me to live, the more He reveals to me about Himself, and the more clearly I can see Him :)

Update – January 27, 2020

Just a little something I remember from a Joyce Meyer teaching. I don't remember it exactly, but it was something to the effect that it takes effort to achieve important and/or useful things in life. It takes little or no effort to achieve unhealthy and/or sinful things. For example, you can get sick without trying; you can gain weight without trying; you can be unkind and hateful without trying very hard. On the other hand, it takes effort to exercise, to be kind, to be patient, to restrain from overindulging. The things that are good for us in life require some effort on our part. The same is true for our relationship with God. It does not just happen automatically. We have to put some effort into it!

Taking Care of Your Temple
Journal Entry   30 June 2015
Blog Entry   31 January 2020

Read over Hebrews 6 again today. I haven't been feeling well lately. I realized that I need to get back on track with eating properly and exercising. These are the basics, the underlying truths for my life, that will keep my body and mind strong and will give me the good foundation I need to grow spiritually. I can't grow spiritually when I'm not taking good care of my body. This just really gets in the way for me. Other people probably have other issues or sins that stunt their spiritual growth, but for me, it's overeating and not exercising.

God, please help me get my earthly temple back in order

so that I may learn more about you and my spiritual eyes can open to see new things. Help me get these basics under control so I can move on to the more advanced things you have for me to do in this world.

He who neglects and ignores instruction and discipline despises himself,
But he who learns from rebuke acquires understanding [and grows in wisdom]. (Proverbs 15:32 AMP)

Update - 28 July 2017

I retired from my government job on my 55th birthday, April 10, 2017. I had been clearly hearing God calling me to get my physical self into better shape for years and years. I committed to myself that when I retired, I would make exercise my priority. It's now been 18 weeks since I retired, and I have been exercising three to five times a week, every week, except for two weeks when I was really sick. I started slow with the recumbent bike as that's all I could do, but then moved on to the Elliptical (10 mins each session) and got started on the beginner track. Now, I'm up to 45 minutes at level 5 difficultly. I also do some strength training immediately following my Elliptical workouts.

It definitely requires discipline to keep going. Most days, I don't feel like doing it, but I'm committed to keeping it going, so I do it. I have only lost about 8 pounds so far, but I am definitely feeling stronger, healthier, and definitely better about myself. I think that overeating and not exercising was blocking my spiritual growth. This sin of gluttony created a barrier in my life. That's just for me though, for other people, it would be other things, but for me, that's the piece that I needed to give to God. The piece I want to hold onto but that I can't hold back from God if I want to grow spiritually.

This new discipline in my life brings to mind another discipline the Lord called me to a few years ago, tithing. We are tithing regularly now, and getting that discipline established broke the hold money had on us. We no longer live in fear of running out of money or not having enough. We completely trust God with it. Disciplines are not easy, and it is often a mind game and struggle to get on track. Even when we fail from time to time, it's important to be persistent and keep trying. I feel that by doing these things, giving up these things that we would rather do, and doing the things we know are the right things to do, we give a little more of ourselves over to God. When we give more to Him, it opens up the door for Him to trust us with more of Him. Less of me, old me, and more of you in my life God!

Update - 31 January 2020

God has such amazing timing! Today, I needed to read these notes from years ago to get re-motivated and encouraged to keep on doing the good things. I kept exercising after retiring, and by the Fall of 2018, I was doing 150 minutes per week of exercise pretty consistently. I also made it through the Daniel Fast two years in a row now (January 2019 and January 2020). Throughout all that, I managed to lose 50 lbs! I'm hoping to lose another 50, which would bring me to a more normal weight for my height.

Persistence and consistency are definitely the keys to success. I still don't feel much like eating right and exercising, but I know this is what I am called to do. I need to keep these disciplines up for the rest of my life to stay in proper balance. Thank you, God, for loving me so much that you provide the discipline I need to be the best me.

Grasping the Amazing Gift Jesus Died to Give Us

Journal Entry   2 July 2015
Blog Entry   3 February 2020

Christ's sacrifice once and for all! Hebrews 10 is such an awesome chapter. I highly recommend you sit quietly, read it, and soak it in! This chapter talks about the Old Covenant and the New Covenant. Under the Old Covenant, the sacrifice of blood from animals was required to cleanse the people from their sins. On the Day of Atonement, once a year, the High Priest could enter the Most Holy Place in the Temple. This special place in the Temple, "The Holy of Holies", contained the Ark of the Covenant. The High Priest would enter this secret place, once a year, behind the curtain and offer sacrifices for the people. The High Priest was the only one allowed in this place, and only allowed in there once a year. Animal sacrifices were also offered daily in the outer part of the Temple.

Sins were Never Completely Forgiven Under the Old Covenant

It is important to realize, though, that under the Old Covenant, sins were never completely forgiven. The people had to continue rituals of sacrifices, and each time they made their sacrifice, they were reminded of their sins. They had to keep atoning for their sins over and over.

The New Covenant – One Sacrifice that Covers All Sin Forever

In contrast to that old system of Covenant with God came the New Covenant God made with humanity through the sacrifice of His Son Jesus. Under the New Covenant, our sins are forgiven once and for all by the sacrifice of Jesus' blood. This also means that we don't have to keep reminding ourselves of our failings and feel guilty or ashamed. Christ made the sacrifice once and for all to set us completely free. All we need to do is accept this free gift of forgiveness!

I need to learn how to fully embrace this concept! I need to feel completely free every day so that I can honour Christ's sacrifice. He gave it all for me, so I need to grab hold of that, of all He's done for me, and live this life of freedom and abundance that He has made available to me. It is all here, all free. I just need to get my mind in that space and stop living under condemnation in my mind. It's a mind game the enemy plays with us, and we need to break free from that negative mindset that we can't have it all. Of course, we can! Jesus paid for it all, in full, nothing held back!

On Having Faith and Being Rewarded
Journal Entry   3 July 2015
Blog Entry   5 February 2020

Hebrews 11 is the "Faith Chapter", and refers to many of the most faithful people in the Bible, such as Enoch, Noah, Abraham, Moses, and Rahab. What struck me in reading it today was verse 6.

And it is impossible to please God without faith. Anyone who wants to come to him must believe that God exists and that he rewards those who sincerely seek him. (Hebrews 11:6 NLT)

Of course, that makes sense and is true. If you don't have faith, you won't believe in God because He is unseen. You must trust through faith that He exists. Also interesting is the statement that you must believe He rewards those who sincerely seek Him. This is something I struggle with. I think it's more honourable to serve God purely because it is right and not for a reward. However, I admit that my selfish human nature does look for and desire rewards.

Dear God, help me serve and love you, my Father in Heaven, just for who You are and not for what I will receive, but please don't leave me in need or in want. I do so want to be abundantly blessed, but I also want to honour You as I should, even if there was no reward. This is the tension I live in.

While I wrestle with these thoughts today, thank you for bringing to my mind my current situation with my family. Thank you for helping me see that I am not only helping the family member because I promised my dying Father that I would, but also because it's just the right thing to do. Thank you for removing that "reward" type of condemnation from my mind.

If I'm honest, I must admit that I definitely have an expectation that I will eventually inherit something from the family estate, as I have been told that for years, but that's not why I do it. Thank you for helping me see my true heart on this. Help me not to be so hard on myself and see that my heart is true in serving, whether it leads to a reward of some kind or not, that I would still do it anyway. Thank you for revealing that condemnation type of thinking that the enemy is always pushing in my face.

Update - 31 July 2017

I realize that I generally do feel overwhelmingly compelled to do the right thing. The thought just occurred to me that perhaps that's You're Spirit working in me, pushing me to do the right thing. Perhaps that's not me, that by myself, left alone in my flesh, I wouldn't feel compelled to do what is right. This actually makes You more real to me, that You are, and always have been, operating within me.

That all the good things I desire to do, are actually You inside of me bringing those things to my mind and pushing me in the direction to do them. You have always been working in me. When people have said that "I" am good, a good kind person, I have always thought that was me, was part of who "I" was. In reality though, I think that left on my own, I am not thoughtful or kind. It is Your Spirit alive in me that makes me this way. When I am selfish, unkind, and angry, that's when I have lost sight of Your Spirit in me; that's when I begin to spiral into darkness.

If You Keep the Faith, You Win!
Journal Entry   4 July 2015
Blog Entry   7 February 2020

Right after all the stories of the people of great faith in Hebrews 11:4-31, Hebrews 11:32-35 tells us how God shut the mouths of lions and made a way for his children to escape what was certain death. That's the part I remember, that they trusted God and they won!

By faith these people overthrew kingdoms, ruled with justice, and received what God had promised them. They shut the mouths of lions, ³⁴ quenched the flames of fire, and escaped death by the edge of the sword. Their weakness was turned to strength. They became strong in battle and put whole armies to flight. ³⁵ Women received their loved ones back again from death. (Hebrews 11:32-35 NLT)

However, if you keep reading, it also speaks of those who didn't win, who suffered and were killed for their faith. Their faith was strong enough that they would give everything for their belief in God, even their lives.

But others were tortured, refusing to turn from God in order to be set free. They placed their hope in a better life after the resurrection. ³⁶ Some were jeered at, and their backs were cut open with whips. Others were chained in prisons. ³⁷ Some died by stoning, some were sawed in half,[d] and others were killed with the sword. Some went about wearing skins of sheep and goats, destitute and oppressed and mistreated. ³⁸ They were too good for this world, wandering over deserts and mountains, hiding in caves and holes in the ground. (Hebrews 11:35-38 NLT)

Faith - Simply Trusting God Every Day is the Endgame

It struck me while reading all this that faith is the key no matter the outcome. So even if you don't achieve the thing you think God called you to, the reward you thought you'd get, just keeping faith daily is the endgame, the goal; it is what is required of you. If you keep your faith until the end of your life, you will have won.

Simply being faithful, lovingly working to serve God every day means you've achieved the goal for your life, no matter what is happening around you in the physical world. As long as you pursue that relationship every day, your life will be well-lived, no matter what it looks like in the physical world. No matter what others think of you. No matter what you think others think of you. You have met your life goal each day that you stay in close relationship with God and listen to the leading of His Holy Spirit.

Drop Your Baggage and Run Free
Journal Entry   6 July 2015
Blog Entry   12 February 2020

I might camp out in Hebrews 12 for a few days because it is so packed with important truths and statements that I could almost be captured to write at length about every couple of verses! Right off the bat, Hebrews 12:1-3 is so impactful for me.

Therefore, since we are surrounded by such a huge crowd of witnesses *to the life of faith, let us strip off every weight that slows us down, especially the sin that so easily trips us up. And let us run with endurance the race God has set before us. ^{2} We do this by keeping our eyes on Jesus, the champion who initiates and perfects our faith. (Hebrews 12:1-3 NLT)*

I've found this to be so true! When I intentionally let go of the things weighing me down, fight off the sinful desires and thoughts, and put the Lord first in my day and first in my mind, then I run this life race in a beautiful way. My mind thinks in new ways, and my senses experience things more deeply. I even recall happy childhood memories! There is a beauty, a freshness to life that is difficult for me to explain in words. My mind and thoughts are renewed, refreshed, cleansed from the stagnation of trudging through life. There is a freshness, a refreshing sense of how beautiful and wonderful this life race can be.

You are Invited to the Family of God

Journal Entry   7 July 2015
Blog Entry   15 February 2020

You have come to, are a part of, the Assembly of God's firstborn children whose names are written in Heaven.

^{18} You have not come to a physical mountain, to a place of flaming fire, darkness, gloom, and whirlwind, as the Israelites did at Mount Sinai. ^{19} For they heard an awesome trumpet blast and a voice so terrible that they begged God to stop speaking. ^{20} They staggered back under God's command: "If even an animal touches the mountain, it must be stoned to death." ^{21} Moses himself was so frightened at the sight that he said, "I am terrified and trembling." ^{22} No, you have come to Mount Zion, to the city of the living God, the heavenly Jerusalem, and to countless thousands of angels in a joyful gathering. ^{23} You have come to the assembly of God's firstborn children, whose names are written in heaven. You have come to God himself, who is the judge over all things. (Hebrews 12:18-23 NLT)

Verses 18 to 21 talk about the Israelites coming to the mountain and God's voice being so terrifying that no one could come near or approach the mountain or they would die. Even Moses was afraid. However, in this age, we have been given the gift of Jesus as our envoy, so we no longer need to fear God. Our choice to accept Jesus as our Saviour has given us the gift of having our names written in Heaven. We are invited into this Assembly as one of God's children, along with the heavenly angels rejoicing over us. We are chosen, special, redeemed. I need to remember this in order to truly grasp who I am in Christ. And it isn't about feeling better than others; this isn't a competitive type of special. It's an individual realization to grab onto and hold tightly to. This invitation is open to anyone who chooses to receive Jesus into their life.

Don't Let Roots of Bitterness Grow
Journal Entry   10 July 2015
Blog Entry   17 February 2020

As the writer wraps up Hebrews, in Chapters 12 and 13, he leaves us with many quick statements that are filled with promise. Instructions that we should follow in order to live our best life.
One that particularly caught my eye was 12:15.

Look after each other so that none of you fails to receive the grace of God. Watch out that no poisonous root of bitterness grows up to trouble you, corrupting many. (Hebrews 12:15 NLT)

We have to continually be on guard and not allow the root of bitterness toward others to grow within us. We need to keep our eyes fixed on Jesus and receive His power so that we may have grace for others. He will allow us to bear things we could not bear in our own humanness. We need to remember to ask Jesus for help as we feel bitterness start to grow in us. If we let bitterness grow, we not only damage our own life walk, but we will also poison others and make them stumble.

Update - 3 August 2017

As I learn to walk closer with God, I have become very aware that God has placed His spirit in me, as He has in everyone, but it is up to us to receive and allow that Spirit to work. It is up to us to let God's Spirit direct our paths and our decisions.

I've started to recognize when my humanness, or my flesh, is thinking thoughts and/or is about to make a decision contrary to God's Spirit. The Holy Spirit suddenly shows up and starts to work in my mind with a conflicting position to the choice I was about to make. I'm learning to yield to God's way instead of my way. I have started to regularly say out loud, "more of you and less of me." I'm starting to understand that in order to live the best life we can live, we need to give Christ, the spirit of God inside of us, control over our decisions and over our thinking. When we do this, Jesus lives out into the world through us. It's still us, our bodies, talents, minds, but with His direction working in us.

The more we yield to Him, the better we live our lives. I guess that's what the scriptures that talk about being "dead to self" are trying to express. Our desires and wants no longer live in us. We live the life Jesus died to give us, which is a life directed by the spirit of God. A life of giving and loving others in the world, following the example of Jesus and how He lived His life.

Just another thought on this: if we don't give God's Spirit control or yield to the spirit of God, then we allow the enemy of our souls, the evil spirits in the world, to guide our thinking. Following the enemy's guidance will only lead to death and destruction. The Devil is a liar, is very sneaky, and the master at tricking us into thinking that we should be in control of our own thinking. The truth is that if we are not allowing God's spirit to lead us, then we are giving the enemy power over us. We need to understand that spiritually we don't have any power on our own. There are only two options: God's way or the Devil's way. Our enemy, the Devil, tricks us into thinking we can reject God and get along just fine. He makes us think we have control over our lives, but it's a lie. If we are rejecting God, the enemy is controlling us, and this path will lead to death.

God Invites Us Into the Unshakeable Kingdom
Journal Entry   11 July 2015
Blog Entry   19 February 2020

"Yet once more I will shake not only the earth but also the heavens." ^{27} This phrase, "Yet once more," indicates the removal of things that are shaken—that is, things that have been made—in order that the things that cannot be shaken may remain. ^{28} Therefore let us be grateful for receiving a kingdom that cannot be shaken, and thus let us offer to God acceptable worship, with reverence and awe. (Hebrews 12:26-28 ESV)

We shouldn't be worried or preoccupied about the shakeable things in our lives. Things like money, clothes, possessions, these things are really so minor and not worth worrying about in the light of what God is giving us.
Jesus died to open the door for us to enter the Unshakeable Kingdom! We need to divert our time and effort from the shakeable things of the world and focus on the unshakeable, our faith, and our relationship with Jesus and our Father God. When we put our trust in Jesus, we will be safely tethered as the final shaking of this world takes place. When all worldly things are stripped away, we

will inherit the Unshakable eternal Kingdom our Father has prepared for us!

Valuable Instructions
Journal Entry   16 July 2015
Blog Entry   22 February 2020

In the final chapter of Hebrews, the writer gives us a list of instructions. Hebrews 13:1-17 offers us some guidelines to live by, statements of huge value and significant truth! Just an amazing list of important useful instructions, all in one place! I've listed a few of them here.

13:2 Don't forget to show hospitality to strangers, for some who have done this have entertained angels.

13:3 Remember those in prison as if you were there yourself. Remember also those being mistreated as if you felt their pain in your own body.

13:4 Give honour to marriage.

13:5 Do not love money, and be content with what you have. God promised to never abandon us. Be satisfied with what God has given you.

13:6 We can say with confidence, the Lord is my helper, whom shall I fear! (What can mere mortal men do to me)

13:8-9 Jesus Christ is the same yesterday, today, and forever, so don't be attracted by strange new spiritual ideas.

13:9 Your strength comes from God's grace!

13:14 This world is not our permanent home.

13:15 Continually praise God through Jesus and show allegiance to His name.

13:16 Do good and share with those in need.

13:17 Obey spiritual leaders and do what they say. Their calling is to watch over you.

12
THE BOOK OF JAMES

See Problems as an Opportunity to Watch God Work
Journal Entry   16 July 2015
Blog Entry   24 February 2020

When troubles of any kind come your way, consider it an opportunity for great joy. For you know that when your faith is tested, your endurance has a chance to grow. So let it grow, for when your endurance is fully developed, you will be perfect and complete, needing nothing. (James 1:2-4 NLT)

James tells us the attitude we should have when trials and challenges come our way. We shouldn't reject them, or be angry and frustrated with them, but see them in a positive light as an opportunity to grow. When we look at our troubles this way and engage the Lord to help us find our way through them, we will find ourselves stronger on the other side of the trial.

We should never think of ourselves as victims when difficulties confront us, but as victorious! We have God with us, inside us, and nothing is impossible for our God who loves us and promises to never leave us or forsake us. Our God is always working things out for the good of those who love Him. When trouble comes our way, we need to keep our eyes steadily fixed on Him. Then we won't fall into believing lies that tell us we can't overcome, endure, and emerge victorious!

Easy to Say, Hard to Do. Update - 24 Feb 2020

I realize that embracing difficulties and problems as a positive is not easy! Just last week, I was in a minor car accident, and I certainly struggled in the first few hours after the accident to see anything positive about it! My mind was reeling and I was overcome with many emotions, none of them very positive. However, I did experience some supernatural emotional strength to remain peaceful. I think it's very helpful to pre-position ourselves to realize that troubles will come in life but that God will help us through them all. If we posture our hearts this way, then in the moment of trial, it is easier for us to remember to cry out to God and know that He is with us and will strengthen us.

In my case, a few days after the accident, while sitting in the repair shop, reading a Joyce Meyer book, the Lord dropped some totally awesome revelations into my mind. Ideas that will help me fight some battles I'm currently fighting. Perhaps going through the accident allowed me to see things differently, and therefore allowed me to see some of the things God was trying to show me. I know that I definitely emerged stronger in faith after the accident.

Un-Divided Loyalty
Journal Entry   17 July 2015
Blog Entry   2 March 2020

If you need wisdom, ask our generous God, and he will give it to you. He will not rebuke you for asking. ⁶ But when you ask him, be sure that your faith is in God alone. Do not waver, for a person with divided loyalty is as unsettled as a wave of the sea that is blown and tossed by the wind. ⁷ Such people should not expect to receive anything from the Lord. ⁸ Their loyalty is divided between God and the world, and they are unstable in everything they do. (James 1:5-8 NLT)

We need to trust God to satisfy all our needs and not strive to do things in our own strength. It is often hard to discern if we are doing this or not. We need to keep our eyes fixed on Jesus, trust and be obedient to the word, then trust that we will receive all God has for us.

God is the solid rock, the same yesterday, today, and forever. He will not leave or forsake you. Believe that., really believe that. Have that abounding hope that He will work out everything for your good, even when it looks hopeless through your human eyes. Keep trusting, keep standing on the solid rock of your creator, the lover of your soul, and the one for whom nothing is impossible! Since God is for you, rejoice in that victory! Even if you can't yet see it in the flesh.

What is My Purpose and Motivation?
Journal Entry   18 July 2015
Blog Entry   4 March 2020

It's Saturday morning, and I've told the family that I really need some quiet time, my time alone with God before I come down for breakfast and dig into the day. I'm starting not to feel so selfish in doing that. I'm starting to realize that maybe I'm allowed to set up a few boundaries. Otherwise, I just feel worn out and exhausted, and no one likes a worn out and exhausted mommy.

But I definitely have to fight feelings of guilt over this time to myself. Feelings that I'm just not doing it quite right if I'm not giving everything I have to my family. I feel like that's my purpose, to take care of my family. But maybe my purpose is more than that. So that thought just felt wrong as well. It's as if anything I do that is not connected to serving my kids, or husband, or even extended family, is selfish. My feelings tell me that I should be using up all of myself for that, and if I'm not, it seems selfish. Weird realization that is! I'll ponder that one! Help me, Holy Spirit, to change my thinking and perception on this if it's not in line with Your plans and what You want me to do in this life.

Why Do I Spend Time with God?
This morning I'm also thinking about my motivation of devoting a prayer and Bible reading time with God each morning. I felt called last October (2014) to begin doing this, and it has since become a habit now that I look forward to. But lately, I've been questioning my motivation here as well. Why am I doing this? Is it because I want things? Is it out of selfish motivation? I was starting to worry that maybe I was doing this for the wrong reasons. But when I examined my heart on it this morning, I came to the realization that I've formed this habit in response to my genuine faith and hope in God. Deep in my being, I have a rock-solid faith in the idea that I was created by God, that He created me for a purpose and a reason, that He has a plan for my life that is much better and more fulfilling than anything I could plan for myself. I want to live out His plan, not mine, because His is so much better than mine, and it is the honourable thing to do. After all, He created me and sent His son to die for me so that I could be reunited with Him at the end of my time here on earth. He also released the Holy Spirit so that I could be guided and directed by the plan God has for me. In the end, I believe that my motivation is good and not greedy or false.

Thank You!
Thank you, Holy Spirit, for helping me see clearly today, and thank you for creating me, Father, and for teaching me the way to live every day by your Holy Spirit. Thank you, Jesus, for Your teaching and the sacrifice of Your life that allows me to have this knowledge, wisdom, and freedom. Not to mention taking away all fear of death! I'm beginning to learn to love You. I remember that I had prayed about this years ago. I didn't know how to love you, Jesus. You seemed distant and untouchable, so it was

hard to form that relationship, but I believe I'm starting to get closer to understanding how to love You. Thank you for initiating and drawing me into this relationship with you!

Catch Those Tempting Thoughts Before They Grow Into Sin
Journal Entry   20 July 2015
Blog Entry   9 March 2020

This part of James talks about being tempted to do wrong, to do what you know is not the right thing to do. James explains that when you are tempted, it's not God that is tempting you; only good things come from God, not bad or evil things. So, if you are tempted to do something that is not good for you or others, this desire is coming from your own human flesh. The desire starts in your mind, and if you don't catch it and rebuke it at that point, it may grow into an action. If you act on that thought you knew was wrong, that action is a sin, and those sins keep piling up and eventually destroy your spirit.

And remember, when you are being tempted, do not say, "God is tempting me." God is never tempted to do wrong,[c] and he never tempts anyone else. ¹⁴ Temptation comes from our own desires, which entice us and drag us away. ¹⁵ These desires give birth to sinful actions. And when sin is allowed to grow, it gives birth to death. (James 1:13-15 NLT)

The message from James is that we need to catch those thoughts and refrain from acting on them. Don't think they are coming from God. God is there to help you overcome them!

Don't Just Listen to God's Word - Do It!
Journal Entry   21 July 2015

Blog Entry   12 March 2020

But don't just listen to God's word. You must do what it says. Otherwise, you are only fooling yourselves. [23] For if you listen to the word and don't obey, it is like glancing at your face in a mirror. [24] You see yourself, walk away, and forget what you look like. (James 1:22-23 NLT)

The Lord gave us His words and His wisdom in the Bible. Not to just read it and think, oh, that's good, that's what we should do, or that's a good story. He gave it to us so that we could actively engage these ideas in living our lives. He wants us to use this wisdom, taking hold of this guidance for our lives and living it out.

It is definitely a battle every day. I don't know yet if it gets easier, but as Joyce Meyer says, at least I'm making progress. I'm not there yet, where I want to be, and where I feel God is calling me to be, but I'm definitely making progress!

Religion that is pure and undefiled before God the Father is this: to visit orphans and widows in their affliction, and to keep oneself unstained from the world. (James 1:27 ESV)

God's Plane and the World's Plane
Journal Entry   22 July 2015
Blog Entry   13 March 2020

Understand this, my dear brothers and sisters: You must all be quick to listen, slow to speak, and slow to get angry. [20] Human anger does not produce the righteousness God desires. [21] So get rid of all the filth and evil in your lives, and humbly accept the word God has planted in your hearts, for it has the power to save your souls.
(James 1:19-21 NLT)

Wow, this passage is so packed, loaded with food for our minds and souls. It's like there are two planes or paths we can be on in our life on this earth. There is the Godly plane and the worldly plane. Of course, the worldly plane is easy to find and easy to step into. It's the plane, or level, that most of us live on each day of our lives. We go through our day with envy, bitterness, selfishness, jealousy, competitiveness, slander, bad language, unkind thoughts, etc. This is the way of the world, and the usual course humans follow or slip into. Some may try to be kind to others here and there, so a little Godliness breaks through into our worldly living now and then.

James is telling us that there is a completely different plane we can live on. We can live in this world on the Godly plane where there is no bitterness, anger, jealousy, selfishness. When we live on this plane, it's that whole concept of living in the world but not being of the world.

God Has Set You Apart, So Lift Yourself Out of the Pit

When we aren't on God's plane, worldliness dominates every action of our lives so that we aren't even aware of it in most cases. However, it is possible to separate ourselves out of that squalor and filthy existence. It is possible to intentionally remove the filth from our thinking, speaking, and actions, and conduct ourselves in the way we know to be true and right. We know what is right from the truth God has planted in our hearts. If we will intentionally tear ourselves free of the regular way of behaving in our culture and behave in a Godly manner, we will experience true freedom and blessing in our lives. If we will walk humbly with our God and put away all boastfulness and pride, we will be living on God's plane. It seems opposite to what we think we should do, but it is the true way to live a life that honours God.

Dear God, please help me recognize the filth in my life and get rid of it. Help me live a clean life that honours you!

The Law That Sets Us Free?
Journal Entry   23 July 2015
Blog Entry   16 March 2020

So whatever you say or whatever you do, remember that you will be judged by the law that sets you free. (James 2:12 NLT)
The law that sets you free? Such a loaded statement! Just a few words but packed with so much meaning. How can the law set you free when it is the law you are being judged against?

If we didn't have the law, we wouldn't know what God's standard is, and therefore we wouldn't know that we are guilty of sin. But since we have the law, we know we are guilty, for it is impossible to keep the law. (Note, the law in Old Testament times was not only the 10 Commandments but all the laws set out in Leviticus. There were many, many rules the Jewish people were to follow). However, none of us can even keep the 10 Commandments!

Have you failed to put God first in your life every day? Have you ever told a lie? Have you ever been envious and wanted what someone else had? I know I am guilty of all these things and more!

Since we know we are guilty, then we know we need a Saviour and we cling to our Saviour Jesus Christ who sets us free. If we didn't have the law, we wouldn't know we were guilty and in need of a Saviour. We would be trapped in our wrongdoing. We would be condemned to bondage in our shortcomings and mistakes, and we would eventually experience spiritual death. Praise God that He has made a way for us hopeless humans and given us hope in Jesus!

Faith and Good Works

Journal Entry   24 July 2015
Blog Entry   18 March 2020

In James 2:14-26, we are offered an explanation by James of how faith in Jesus leads to good works in the world. James says that you don't have faith if you aren't doing good works. I believe there has been a lot of misunderstanding around this passage to the effect that you must do good works to be saved – that your salvation depends on your good works. What an untruth!

Jesus Already Did All the Work. You Cannot Earn Salvation!

It's unfortunate that people think James is saying that you must do good works in the world to be saved. Thinking this can totally skew their understanding of how loving God is. Jesus did all the work for our salvation; we don't have to do any good works to earn it!

The Natural Outflow of True Faith in Jesus is Good Works

What James is saying is that if you have genuine, true faith in God and in his son Jesus, your life will end up producing good works. It is the natural outflow of true faith in God. You don't have to try to do good works; they just flow out of you when you have a right relationship with God. It is impossible to have a right relationship with God and not produce good works in your life. This doesn't mean you will be perfect all the time, it is a process, but goodness begins to flow out of you when you have genuine faith and a right relationship with God. When you have faith, the fruit of that faith is good works.

What About Good Works Without Faith?

The sad part is that you can also produce good works without faith and think this will save you from hell. However, you can't be saved by works alone. You can't earn your salvation. It's impossible to meet God's standard! That's why Jesus came to earth and died for us. Our culture is very confused in this area. They believe good works alone are the right thing, and they don't really need God. The reverse is true! They need the relationship with God first, and the good works will flow out of that. Our spiritual enemy, Satan, has fooled us into thinking that doing good things and being a good person is enough, so much so that we don't need a relationship with God. The Devil is happy with you doing good works. He doesn't mind you doing good works because you belong to him all this time and will belong to him in the end. That's his objective, to steal away as many souls as he can from God, their creator.

Your Words Are So Important
Journal Entry   27 July 2015
Blog Entry   20 March 2020

People can tame all kinds of animals, birds, reptiles, and fish, [8] but no one can tame the tongue. It is restless and evil, full of deadly poison. [9] Sometimes it praises our Lord and Father, and sometimes it curses those who have been made in the image of God. [10] And so blessing and cursing come pouring out of the same mouth.
(James 3:1-12 NLT)

The importance of the tongue (your words). It is important, more important than we know, to control what we say. If we are putting others down or joking about others, we are decreasing the blessings God can give us. We are actually assisting the enemy of our souls when we use our words to say things we know we shouldn't, about others or about circumstances. We need to be more intentional about what we say and what we don't say, more disciplined in our speech.

Father God, please help me to be more aware of my words

and to use my gift of speech for good! Amen.

Update - 20 March 2020

The words we say are so important! These include words we say about ourselves, even the unuttered ones. I remember a teaching from Joyce Meyer on this topic. She told us the loudest voice our minds hear about ourselves is what we say about ourselves. We will start to believe whatever it is we say about ourselves. Therefore, it's critical to not say negative things about yourself! Just don't do it! You are a child of God, created in God's image for a specific purpose and mission in the world. You matter, and God loves you more than you can ever realize. He will give you what you need if you rest in Him and trust Him.

Recently we have gone through a season at home wherein our teenage daughter shouts out negative things about herself while during her homework. Every time she makes the slightest error or doesn't immediately understand something, she yells out how stupid she is. This drives me crazy because I see that she is falling into the enemy's lies in this scenario. At a recent women's conference I attended, the Lord gave me a new weapon for these situations. He told me to counter the enemy's lie with the truth each time she says one of these things. For example, if she shouts out, "I'm stupid!" we should say clearly out loud, "that's a lie from the enemy. You are very intelligent, and that's why the enemy wants you to think otherwise." When we expose the enemy this way, throw the light onto the lie, he flees! It works so well!

Jealousy and Selfishness
Journal Entry   29 July 2015
Blog Entry   23 March 2020

For wherever there is jealousy and selfish ambition, there you will find disorder and evil of every kind. (James 3:16 NLT)

James tells us that jealousy and selfishness are not of God; they are demonic. He teaches us that true wisdom that comes from God allows us to live out our lives doing good works in peacefulness and kindness. If we are full of jealousy and selfishness, we haven't yet learned God's ways.

Two Options for Living Life; Which Will You Choose?

Journal Entry   30 July 2015
Blog Entry   25 March 2020

You adulterers! Don't you realize that friendship with the world makes you an enemy of God? I say it again: If you want to be a friend of the world, you make yourself an enemy of God.
(James 4:4-5 NLT)

Here again, I see James keeping in his theme that there are two ways to live. You can live in the world quarrelling, fighting, being jealous, angry, unkind, full of gossip, or you can live on God's plane. You will still live in the same world, but as you draw closer and closer to God, intentionally pursue Him, He will draw closer to you. You will begin to hear the Holy Spirit gently guiding you and directing you in the paths of righteousness, the path in God's plane. The Holy Spirit nudges but doesn't force you. You have to intentionally desire to walk in the direction He is directing you to walk. He has a better plan and a better life for you, but it all seems harder to you. The enemy makes it look undesirable, so you have to break through all the junk of this world and cling to that path. This will result in the truly abundant life you were meant to have! If you don't do this, you will continue to live a substandard, unfulfilled life.

It's Sin to Do It When You Know You Shouldn't
Journal Entry   31 July 2015
Blog Entry   27 March 2020

Humble yourself before God, resist the Devil and he will flee from you. (James 4:7 NLT)

It is sin to know what you ought to do and then not do it. (James 4:17 NLT)

These are such powerful statements to me. I know I shouldn't overeat or overspend, or swear, or gossip, or complain. So, when I give in to these things that I know I shouldn't do, then I am sinning. God forgives me, of course, but when I fill my life with sin, I am allowing the enemy to take away blessings and joy that God wants to give me. God still blesses me with many things, but I would be even more blessed if I didn't allow the enemy to rule my life!

Update - 27 March 2020

God's perfect timing! I so needed to be reminded of this today, particularly as we go through this whole COVID 19 Pandemic and all the changes and challenges in our lives. The Lord has actually blessed me so abundantly during this time! I do have more than everything I need to get through this time, but I need to restrain myself from overindulging in food and underusing my physical body! I need to remember that it is a sin to overeat and stop doing that! Thank you, Lord, for this amazing reminder today! Thank you that you are so patient with me as I continue to slip up in this area. Thank you that You continue to bring me back to the right path.

What Do You Do with Your Money?
Journal Entry   1 August 2015

Blog Entry   31 March 2020

You have spent your years on earth in luxury satisfying your every desire. You have fattened yourselves for the day of slaughter. (James 5:5 NLT)

I actually took some comfort reading this verse, probably because our bank account is almost always in negative territory. However, we do indulge in many extras, like take-out food, that we could cut down on so that we could be more giving to those in need.

I think about my dad when reading this verse. He died with a great deal of money in the bank, but he was very generous throughout his life and didn't spend much on himself. In fact, he wouldn't even buy a comfortable chair for himself, which we encouraged him to do as his back hurt so much. He didn't want to buy it because it was very expensive and he didn't want to waste that money on himself. He was always thinking of others' needs and how he could help them. He wanted to leave a substantial amount of money to his kids when he died, which he did accomplish. I think that it's not bad or sinful to have a lot of money but what you do with it is very important to God.

Just Do What You Say You'll Do
Journal Entry   4 August 2015
Blog Entry   4 April 2020

But most of all, my brothers and sisters, never take an oath, by heaven or earth or anything else. Just say a simple yes or no, so that you will not sin and be condemned. (James 5:12 NLT)

James 5:12 and Matthew 5:33-37 talk about the same principle. We are to be people of integrity, known for our integrity. Our word is enough without the need to invoke heaven or earth when we make promises or say we're going to do something. If we say we will do it, we should just do it! We shouldn't make grand promises we can't keep. We need to be true to our yes or our no, simply and honestly, without drama and the apparent invocation of some higher power.

"You have also heard that our ancestors were told, 'You must not break your vows; you must carry out the vows you make to the Lord. But I say, do not make any vows! Do not say, 'By heaven!' because heaven is God's throne. And do not say, 'By the earth!' because the earth is his footstool. And do not say, 'By Jerusalem!' for Jerusalem is the city of the great King. Do not even say, 'By my head!' for you can't turn one hair white or black. Just say a simple, 'Yes, I will,' or 'No, I won't.' Anything beyond this is from the evil one. (Matthew 5:33-37 NLT)

Confessing Sins to Each Other
Journal Entry   5 August 2015
Blog Entry   7 April 2020

Confess your sins to each other and pray for each other so that you may be healed. The earnest prayer of a righteous person has great power and produces wonderful results. (James 5:16 NLT)

This passage caught my eye this morning, probably because of the difference between the Catholic and Protestant churches when it comes to confession. The study notes in my Life Application Bible have really helpful information on this idea of confessing our sins. It offers the following:

- If we have sinned against someone, we need to confess our sin to them and ask for their forgiveness.
- If our sin has affected the church, we must confess it publicly to those affected.

- If we need loving support as we struggle with a sin, we should confess the sin to those we trust who can support us in this area.
- If we doubt God's forgiveness for a specific sin, we may want to confess it to a fellow believer for assurance of God's pardon.

Finally, the Study Bible concludes this area with the following statement: "In Christ's Kingdom, every believer is a priest to other believers." I found this entire section so helpful in understanding the whole idea of confessing sins one to another.

God Still Works Through the Lives of Those Who Choose to Trust Him

Journal Entry   11 August 2015
Blog Entry   10 April 2020

Elijah was as human as we are, and yet when he prayed earnestly that no rain would fall, none fell for three and a half years! [18] *Then, when he prayed again, the sky sent down rain and the earth began to yield its crops. (James 5:17-18 NLT)*

This passage stood out for me today. I thought I was going to start 1st Peter this morning, but my mind just kept steady on the idea that Elijah was as human as we are. I often forget that and think that the Bible Heroes and Prophets that did amazing things were supernatural somehow and not like us. However, we need to remember they *were* just like us, and it was God's power working in them that allowed them to do supernatural things. This same power is the same yesterday, today, and forever, and is available to every single one of us. God wants to raise up a whole new generation of Bible Superheroes. He's looking for those who will sincerely bow to Him!

God is so Much More Than Our Minds Can Understand

I think in this society, and this generation, we think we know everything. But I believe we think we know more than we actually do. We conclude that the people depicted in the Bible were not as educated as we are. We assume that if they had the knowledge we have today, they wouldn't believe in God. However, I don't think we are as smart as we think we are. We fail to realize that God is on a whole different level of intelligence. We think of God in our terms, the way our minds can think of Him because that's as far as our thought, our human minds, can go. I believe God is so much bigger than our human minds can even imagine.

Thank you, God, that even though you are so much smarter, more amazing, loving, and brilliant than I can ever imagine, that you choose to have a relationship with me. Even with all my faults and inadequacies, you choose to be steadfast in loving and forgiving me. Thank you for allowing me to know you, even just a little, and please allow me to love you more and serve you better every day!

Live Out Your Faith by Serving Others
Journal Entry   12 August 2015
Blog Entry   13 April 2020

My Life Application Study Bible has a short but great summary of the book of James at the end of the notes for James. It states that the book of James is all about faith in action. God's Church in the world should look like a bit of heaven on earth. If we truly have faith and believe in the word of God, the Bible, that it will compel us to live out our faith by loving and serving and having compassion for others. Our actions will be what draws others to faith. Forcing people, scolding people, and judging people WILL NOT bring people to Christ. Loving and serving them will. This is the example Jesus set in His time on earth. What drew people to Him was His love and compassion for them. As God's church in the world, this is our mission every day, to love and serve others in our midst.

Update – 25 August 2017

I heard a radio teaching recently about Jesus choosing to show His deity by healing and helping people. It was a spin on Jesus I hadn't thought of before. The suggestion was that He could have shown His power and greatness another way. Just imagine the many ways He could have shown that He had the power of the God of the Universe in Him. He could have destroyed evil things, or parted seas, or caused the sun to stop shining, or any number of other things, but He chose to show us God's power by healing and helping people in need. I think this is what James is telling us to do what Jesus did. To love and serve others, and that's how they will find Jesus.

This confirms to me that my service at the Foodbank, and crocheting of shawls for people in need of comfort, is doing the work James is telling us we should be doing. I feel very much in line with God's plan for me at this point in my life. The Foodbank and shawl work, tithing, keeping myself in the word, honouring God with my life, exercising, and doing my best to keep God first in my mind in all circumstances, makes me feel content that I am in step with the Lord. Not everything around me is perfect and the way I would like it to be, but these are all just peripheral things. Keeping God as my focus and following the Holy Spirit's lead is the most important thing.

ABOUT THE AUTHOR

I am a retired civil servant and mother of four children. I have been married for 37 years. I volunteer in my church and my community. I love music and singing.

My Bumpy Road to Knowing God

Troubles Come Early

My family went to a Baptist Church until I was at least five years old. I have a few wonderful memories of church and Sunday school up until that age. However, our family began to fall apart, and we stopped going to church shortly after that. Alcohol, abusive behaviours, and marriage breakdown overran my parents and became my everyday reality. Dad moved out when I was ten years old, and another abusive man took his place in my mother's life. My life as a teenager was so messed up that I tried to kill myself when I was sixteen. I saw this as the only way out of the circumstances I had found myself in. I felt powerless. By the grace of God, I wasn't successful in my attempt to end it all. My life slowly became more tolerable once I got out on my own a couple of years later. However, at this point in my life, I had very much lost sight of God and didn't even give Him a second thought.

Baptized – God Starts Leading Me Back to Him

In 1983 I was baptized—full immersion—in a Baptist church. This wasn't due to any spectacular spiritual revelation or because I was particularly religious, but because the Catholic priest who was going to preside over my marriage ceremony advised that I couldn't marry my fiancé unless I was baptized. He essentially said that I didn't exist if I wasn't baptized. I was okay with getting baptized but wanted to do it the way I understood from my Baptist upbringing. The Priest would accept that as long as I could provide a Certificate of Baptism. Up until that point, I had never even received communion. I was raised to understand that receiving communion was not allowed until I was baptized. So, at 21 years old, I took a course at the local Baptist church, got baptized, confessed my faith in Jesus publicly, and began to receive Holy communion. However, I was still very far from God playing any kind of role, much less a central role, in my life.

A Voice in the Midst of Dark Times

My husband and I were both looking forward to starting a family. Unfortunately, after a miscarriage and many years of medication and fertility clinic procedures, I found myself at a difficult crossroads. I felt I had to stop all the fertility drugs as my hair was falling out, and I was breaking out in rashes all over my body. I was deeply depressed that we were unable to start the family I so desperately wanted. It was 1989, and as I stood in my kitchen looking out the window and feeling engulfed in a pit of sadness, I heard a voice in my head say, "Go to church." This was such a foreign idea for me at this time. I looked around to see if anyone had said that, but here I stood alone in the kitchen and the only one in the house. I had rarely attended church since I had been baptized six years earlier. At that time, church was reserved for Christmas and Easter.

However, I could not shake this strange experience of hearing that *voice*. As I had no other options left, I decided to go to church and pray for a baby. I started attending a Baptist church and cried at every baby dedication, trying desperately to hide my tears. Sunday after Sunday, I prayed for a child. After about seven months of continued church attendance and prayer, I was astonished and elated to find that I was pregnant. This is when I began to wonder if God was real. I mean, nothing else worked but prayer. Prayer worked. God worked.

My Attempt to Repay

After our first child was born, I felt that I owed God bigtime! But even after all those years of darkness and finally having the baby we wanted so much, seemingly assisted by the power of prayer, I still wasn't completely convinced God existed. Talk about stubborn! However, I was willing to give Him the benefit of the doubt. I told God that I wanted to believe in Him. I felt at that point in my life that I had to make a choice, either take all references and acknowledgment of God and Christianity out of my life or choose to believe. I felt I had to be either fully in or fully out, not just sort of believe for the sake of Christmas and Easter. I said to God that I was choosing to believe in Him but would He please give me faith as I still had a lot of doubt at that time. I began to regularly attend a local church and sing in the choir as I felt that's how I could contribute and give back.

The Beginning of an Amazing Journey

God answered my prayer for more faith. Step by step, day by day, year by year, He revealed more of Himself to me. It wasn't an overnight revelation or anything like that, but as I continued to seek Him, He started to show up in the little things in my life. At first, I would think, God, is that you? Then I'd think no, it was just a coincidence. But over and over, He would show up in the circumstances in my life to the point that I had to stop denying Him and really start to believe He was real. We ended up with three more children, and I have an amazing story of faith for each one, no fertility drugs at all! Since that first call I heard in my kitchen, I've been on this incredible journey of faith. God just keeps showing up everywhere in my life, helping me through hard times and showering me with so many good things. This way of living has become my new normal.

Where Am I Now?
I have been retired from my day job for a over three years now. I worked mostly full time for 36 years. Over the years, I had heard God calling me to give up working outside the home several times, to stay home with the kids, but I kept depending on me, and not on Him. It was very hard to work full-time and be the parent I wanted to be to my kids. I lost most of the hearing in my left ear after an unpleasant incident at work in 2011. Work was definitely wearing me down. God was calling me to a different path, but sadly, my faith still wasn't strong enough to fully rely on God to provide.

When I finally reached the point where I could retire with a good pension, I knew it was definitely time to go and didn't work a single day longer. At that time, we still had a mountain of debt, a mortgage, and two more kids to put through post-secondary education, but I knew I had delayed God's call for too long already, and it was time to go. Now I find myself here, working on my blog page and putting this book together. I know God is continuing to heal and shape my life, and I am so thankful for that!